Mastering
Primary
Science

Mastering Primary Teaching series

Edited by Judith Roden and James Archer

The *Mastering Primary Teaching* series provides an insight into the core principles underpinning each of the subjects of the primary National Curriculum, thereby helping student teachers to 'master' the subjects. This in turn will enable new teachers to share this mastery in their teaching. Each book follows the same sequence of chapters, which has been specifically designed to assist trainee teachers to capitalise on opportunities to develop pedagogical excellence. These comprehensive guides introduce the subject and help trainees know how to plan and teach effective and inspiring lessons that make learning irresistible. Examples of children's work and case studies are included to help exemplify what is considered to be best and most innovative practice in primary education. The series is written by leading professionals, who draw on their years of experience to provide authoritative guides to the primary curriculum subject areas.

Also available in the series

Mastering Primary English, Wendy Jolliffe and David Waugh

Mastering Primary Languages, Paula Ambrossi and Darnelle Constant-Shepherd

Mastering Primary Music, Ruth Atkinson

Mastering Primary Physical Education, Kristy Howells with Alison Carney, Neil Castle and Rich Little

Forthcoming in the series

Mastering Primary Art and Design, Peter Gregory, Claire March and Suzy Tutchell

Mastering Primary Computing, Graham Parton and Christine Kemp-Hall

Mastering Primary Design and Technology, Gill Hope

Mastering Primary Geography, Anthony Barlow and Sarah Whitehouse

Mastering Primary History, Karin Doull, Christopher Russell and Alison Hales

Mastering Primary Mathematics, Andrew Lamb, Rebecca Heaton and Helen Taylor

Mastering Primary Religious Education, Maria James and Julian Stern

Also available from Bloomsbury

Developing Teacher Expertise, edited by Margaret Sangster

Readings for Reflective Teaching in Schools, edited by Andrew Pollard

Reflective Teaching in Schools, Andrew Pollard

Mastering Primary Science

Amanda McCrory and Kenna Worthington

Bloomsbury Academic
An imprint of Bloomsbury Publishing Plc

B L O O M S B U R Y

LONDON · OXFORD · NEW YORK · NEW DELHI · SYDNEY

Bloomsbury Academic

An imprint of Bloomsbury Publishing Plc

50 Bedford Square
London
WC1B 3DP
UK

1385 Broadway
New York
NY 10018
USA

www.bloomsbury.com

**BLOOMSBURY and the Diana logo are trademarks
of Bloomsbury Publishing Plc**

First published 2018

British Library Cataloguing-in-Publication Data
A catalogue record for this book is available from the British Library.

ISBN: HB: 978-1-4742-7744-0
PB: 978-1-4742-7743-3
ePDF: 978-1-4742-7746-4
ePub: 978-1-4742-7745-7

Library of Congress Cataloging-in-Publication Data
A catalog record for this book is available from the Library of Congress.

Series: Mastering Primary Teaching

Cover design by Anna Berzovan
Cover image © iStock (miakievy/molotovcoketail)

Typeset by Deanta Global Publishing Services, Chennai, India
Printed and bound in Great Britain

To find out more about our authors and books visit www.bloomsbury.com. Here you
will find extracts, author interviews, details of forthcoming events and the option
to sign up for our newsletters.

Contents

List of Figures

Series Editors' Foreword

Long and varied experience of working with beginning and experienced teachers in primary schools has informed this series since its conception. Over the last 30 years there have been many changes to practice in terms of teaching and learning in primary and Early Years education. Significantly, since the implementation of the first National Curriculum in 1989 the aim has been to bring best practice in primary education to all state schools in England and Wales. As time has passed, numerous policy changes have altered the detail and emphasis of the delivery of the primary curriculum. However, there has been little change in the belief that in the primary and early years phases of education pupils should receive a broad balanced curriculum based on traditional subjects.

Recent Ofsted subject reports and notably the Cambridge Primary Review indicate, that rather than the ideal being attained, in many schools, the emphasis on English and mathematics has not only depressed the other subjects of the primary curriculum, but has also narrowed the range of strategies used for the delivery of the curriculum. Provision in the amount of time allocated to subject sessions in ITE courses has dramatically reduced which may also account for this narrow diet in pedagogy.

The vision of this series of books was borne out of our many years of experience with student teachers. As a result, we believe that the series is well designed to equip trainee and beginning teachers to master the art of teaching in the primary phase. This series of books aims to introduce current and contemporary practices associated with the whole range of subjects within the Primary National Curriculum and religious education. It also goes beyond this by providing beginning teachers the knowledge and understanding required to achieve mastery of each subject. In doing so, each book in the series highlights contemporary issues such as assessment and inclusion which are key areas that even the most seasoned practitioner is still grappling with in light of the introduction of the new Primary Curriculum. As a results equipped with these texts we believe that students that work in schools and progress onto their NQT year will be able to make a significant contribution to the provision in their school, especially in foundation subjects.

Readers will find great support within each one of these texts. Each book in the series will inform and provide the opportunity for basic mastery of each of the subjects, English, mathematics, science, physical education, music, history, geography, design and technology computing and religious education. Readers can expect to learn much about each of the subjects in the series. They will discover the essence of each subject in terms of its philosophy, knowledge and skills. Readers will also be inspired by the enthusiasm for each subject revealed by the subject authors who are experts in their field. They will discover many and varied strategies for making each subject 'come alive' for their pupils and they should become more confident about teaching across the whole range of subjects represented in the primary and early years curriculum.

Primary teaching in the state sector is characterized by a long history of pupils being taught the whole range of the primary curriculum by one teacher. Although some schools may employ subject specialists to deliver some subjects of the curriculum, notably physical education, music or science for example, it is more usual for the whole curriculum to be delivered to a class by their class teacher. This places a potentially enormous burden on beginning teachers no matter which route they enter teaching. The burden is especially high on those entering through employment based routes and for those who aim to become inspiring primary teachers. There is much to learn!

The term 'mastery' is generally considered to relate to knowledge and understanding of a subject which incorporates the 'how' of teaching as well as the 'what'. Although most entrants to primary teaching will have some experience of the primary curriculum as a pupil, very few will have experienced the breadth of the curriculum may have any understanding of the curriculum which reflects recent trends in teaching and learning within the subject. The primary curriculum encompasses a very broad range of subjects each of which has its own knowledge base, skills and ways of working. Unsurprisingly, very few new entrants into the teaching profession hold mastery of all the interrelated subjects. Indeed for the beginning teacher it may well be many years before full mastery of all aspects of the primary curriculum is achieved. The content of the primary curriculum has changed significantly notably in some foundation subjects such as history and music. So although beginning teachers might hold fond memories of these subjects from their own experience of primary education, the content of the subject may well have changed significantly over time and may incorporate different emphases.

The title of the series, Mastering Primary Teaching, aims to meet the needs of those who, reflecting the desire for mastery of each subject, want to know more. This is a tall order. Nevertheless we believe the pursuit of development should always be rewarded which is why we are delighted to have so many experts sharing their well-developed knowledge and passion for the subjects featured in each text. The vision for this series was to provide support for those who are beginning their teaching career that may not feel fully secure in their subject knowledge, understanding and skill. In addition the vision was to provide a reference point for beginning teachers to always be able to go back to support them in the important art of teaching.

Intending primary teachers, in our experience have a thirst for knowledge about the subject that they will be teaching. They want to 'master' new material and ideas in a range of subjects. They aim to gain as much knowledge as they can of the subjects they will be teaching, some of which they may be unfamiliar with, lacking in confidence about or, quite frankly scared to death because of their perceived lack of familiarity with some subjects and particularly how they are delivered in primary schools. Teaching the primary curriculum can be one of the most rewarding experiences. We believe that this series will help you to unlock the primary curriculum in a way that sees you establish yourself as a confident primary practitioner.

Judith Roden
James Archer
June 2017

How to Use This Book

This book is one of twelve books that together help form a truly innovative series that is aimed to support your development. Each book follows the same format and chapter sequence. There is an emphasis throughout the book on providing information about the teaching and learning of science. You will find a wealth of information within each chapter that will help you to understand the issues, problems and opportunities that teaching the subject can provide you as a developing practitioner in the subject. Crucially, each chapter provides opportunities for you to reflect upon important points linked to your development in order that you may master the teaching of science. As a result, you too can develop your confidence in the teaching of a primary science. There really is something for everyone within each chapter.

Each chapter has been carefully designed to help you to develop your knowledge of the subject systematically and as a result contains key features. Chapter objectives clearly signpost the content of each chapter and these will help you to familiarize yourself with important aspects of the subject and will orientate you in preparation for reading the chapter. The regular 'pause for thought' points offer questions and activities for you to reflect on important aspects of the subject. Each 'pause for thought' provides you with an opportunity to enhance your learning beyond merely reading the chapter. These will sometimes ask you to consider your own experience and what you already know about the teaching of the subject. Others will require you to critique aspects of good practice presented as case studies or research. To benefit fully from reading this text, you need to be an active participant. Sometimes you are asked to make notes on your response to questions and ideas and then to revisit these later on in your reading. While it would be possible for you to skip through the opportunities for reflection or to give only cursory attention to the questions and activities which aim to facilitate deeper reflection than might otherwise be the case we strongly urge you to engage with the 'pause for thought' activities. It is our belief that it is through these moments that most of your transformational learning will occur as a result of engaging in this book. At the end of each chapter, you will find a summary of main points from the chapter along with suggestions for further reading are made.

We passionately believe that learners of all ages learn best when they work with others, so we would encourage you, if possible to work with another person, sharing your ideas and perspectives. The book also would be ideal for groups study within a university or school setting.

This book has been authored by Amanda McCrory and Kenna Worthington, who are experienced and highly regarded as professionals in their subject area. They are strong voices within the primary science community. By reading this book you will be able to benefit from their rich knowledge, understanding and experience. When using this ensure that you are ready to learn from some of the greats in primary science.

Introduction

Nothing in life is to be feared, it is only to be understood. Now is the time to understand more, so that we may fear less.

Marie Curie

What do you think education is for? Why do we 'educate' our children, and how, and what place does science have in that education?

If you believe, like us, that one of the purposes of education is to prepare our children for their future, it seems to us that there is a lot about science that can do that. World problems such as climate change, food security, poverty and biodiversity loss will affect the future of our children as they grow up, and some argue that there are no testable solutions to these so-called wicked problems (Fleming and Dillon 2017), but to tackle any one of them needs experts from a number of disciplines working together. If future citizens are going to have a voice in managing these global issues, they need to have the skills and values to think creatively, and that needs to start somewhere.

On a more personal level, science – when taught effectively – has the capacity to equip us with the knowledge and skills needed to make choices in our everyday lives, from the energy that we choose to run our cars and houses, to the medication we might take to enhance our lives. An important aspect of science is innovation; and as a species we have made great strides because of inventions and innovative approaches to problems – creativity is a vital component of this and of being a scientist; primary-aged children are creative and science lessons in primary schools should reflect this.

In primary science education, from Nursery onwards, children will have their starting point. Through our enthusiasm, care and professional practice, their skills in questioning, testing, analysis and evaluation will grow and flourish, giving them the confidence to apply their developing knowledge and understanding of the way the world works to not only enhance their own lives but also to tackle the so-called wicked problems of the world.

This book is **not a reference** for conceptual scientific knowledge; instead one of the main aims of this book is to help you develop *your **teaching pedagogy*** by provoking you to think more deeply about your teaching practice and the issues at hand that you might encounter in school so that you become an effective teacher of science in the primary classroom. This book offers an evidenced informed approach to the teaching, learning and assessment of science in the primary school. Why? To highlight to interested readers best practice in science teaching pedagogy and the challenges that continue to exist in the provision for science in primary schools. The reason for this is simple: to empower teachers, science coordinators and members of leadership teams – in short, anyone who cares about the science education our children receive; to identify what good practice in primary science education in, so that they can implement this in their school setting and consequently to provide the ***absolute best provision of science possible for the children they are accountable for.***

Throughout the book, we have tried to pose questions that will give you pause for thought and a reason to reflect on your own views about science in the primary classroom and what you think that looks like. We do not shy away from highlighting the realities of primary science teaching practice – discussing both the strengths and challenges that primary schools face in their provision for science so that you are equipped to deal with whatever situations arise in relation to this. We have offered case studies from our own students and beginning teachers for you to interrogate and possibly give you ideas for your own practice, and we offer quotes from scientists as well as our own views that we hope will inspire you to be the best teachers of primary science you can be. This, we hope, will bring joy to your practice and a love of learning to your children. There can be no doubt that the aspiration for *all* in the field of science education is to facilitate all children to learn scientific concepts while developing scientific enquiry skills, confidence and a positive attitude to science – enjoying every science session they take part in; this also includes the facilitator of this learning – you need to make sure you are confident and enjoying teaching science to the children you teach! Ultimately, we hope you will be promoting a life long love for learning science for everyone!

We are passionate about children learning science, and we hope that this little book, which comes from our hearts, will convince you too, to be passionate about what science can bring to the education of the children you are privileged to teach!

Amanda McCrory and Kenna Worthington

Chapter 1
An Introduction to Primary Science

All men, by nature, desire to know.

Aristotle

Chapter objectives

By the end of this chapter you will have developed an understanding of:

- What primary science is;
- The nature of science and what this looks like in the primary classroom;
- What it means to be scientific in the primary classroom – what working scientifically means across the primary age range;
- How teaching science can contribute to a child's whole education – taking risks, building resilience and motivation to learn.

Introduction

This chapter is an introduction to primary science which aims to support trainee teachers and teachers to clarify their understanding of science and what science is by firstly discussing the nature of science. Notably that science: endeavours to understand the world and beyond, is a never-ending journey of discovery where scientific ideas change and build on previous ideas and theories; is a global human, endeavour which is inclusive of all different types of people, and perhaps most importantly has changed our lives. The nature of science is then related to primary science education in England and Wales by examining the Science National Curriculum for KS1 and KS2, thus giving the reader an understanding as to what it means to be scientific in the primary classroom, focusing both on process skills (enquiry skills) and conceptual understanding in science lessons. Insights are given here into the integral role social constructivism plays in the primary science classroom; therefore, highlighting the importance of not only teachers' subject knowledge but their pedagogical approaches to teaching science concepts. Finally, there is a discussion about how the effective teaching and learning of primary science contributes to a child's whole education as it enables children to: *explore* which increases creativity and curiosity; develop resilience when taking risks and thus develop a 'growth mindset'; be motivated to learn; transfer skills learnt and practised in science across the curriculum – ultimately, developing young children into scientifically literate individuals.

What is primary science?

As a teacher in a primary school, it is imperative that you have a clear understanding of the scientific content of the national curriculum for science in EYFS, key stages 1 and 2 (and to some extent key stage 3) and how it can be taught effectively (Roden and Archer 2014). At the beginning of every academic year, we ask our students the two questions:

- What is your understanding of the nature science?
- Does it differ from your understanding of primary science?

Both questions ignite considerable debate; therefore, before you read on complete the following pause for thought.

Pause for thought – *What does science mean to you?*

Ask yourself (and be honest):

- When considering what science is, what thoughts and images run through your mind?
- If you had to sum up science in under ten words, what would they be?
- When you hear the word 'science', what is your **emotional reaction** to this and why?
- Do you see a difference between the word science and primary science?
- How confident do you feel in your understanding of conceptual science and working scientifically?

Let us turn initially to the first question: What is science?

When considering what science is, we are contemplating the nature of science. But what is the nature of science? Science takes the view that:

- The world is understandable – that things and events in the universe (a vast single system in which the basic rules apply everywhere) occur in consistent patterns that we come to understand through observation and systematic study. Therefore, scientific inquiry is fundamental to understanding science as it demands evidence to explain observable phenomena.

- Scientific ideas are subject to change – science is a process for producing knowledge; change is inevitable because new observations may challenge prevailing theories and it is important for children to understand that science is not static. Thus, testing, improving and sometimes the discarding of scientific theories is a continual process.

- Scientific knowledge is robust – the norm in science is the modification of ideas, rather than outright rejection, reinforced by scientific evidence until explanations grow more precise and become more widely accepted. Darwin's Theory of Evolution by Natural Selection (1859) is a perfect example of this – Darwin, who was a naturalist, constructed his theory on the basis of his observations of the natural world – he did not 'literally' observe evolution in the making, but observed the similarities and differences in species which helped him to formulate his theory that organisms change over time as a result of physical or behavioural changes. Since then, Evolution by Natural Selection (1859) has been supported by evidence from various different scientific disciplines such as geology and genetics to name but two, arguably making this theory one of the most substantiated in the history of science.

- Science is a complex social activity, involving many individuals undertaking a variety of different roles; diversity invigorates problem-solving, thus science benefits from a community which approaches problem-solving creatively; this in turn also balances biases which might occur if science was only practised by a narrow subset of people.

- Science cannot provide complete answers to all questions – there are many matters which cannot be examined in a scientific way; for example belief in the true purpose of life cannot be proved or disproved.

Which of these points occurred to you when undertaking reflection one? How will you use this knowledge to ensure that you become an effective teacher of science in the primary classroom? Our experience is that when introducing the word 'nature', ambivalence can occur and thus cause anxiety. There is a perception that science is complex, multifaceted and, therefore, only attractive to certain individuals – perhaps this was your thinking? In a way, this does a disservice to the subject and detracts from the most important characteristics of science which are in themselves straightforward.

Of course, science becomes a more complex area of study as children progress to GCSE, A' Level and beyond, and although not as complex at key stages 1 and 2, research evidence tells us that the most effective teachers have a deep knowledge of the subject they teach (Coe et al. 2014) which when it comes to science must therefore include the nature of science as well as how to teach it. Pedagogical Content Knowledge

(Shulman 1986, 2015) underpins effective teaching because it combines multifaceted knowledge (child development, learning theories, teaching strategies including explanations and demonstrations which make abstract principles concrete for children to understand; inclusion and differentiation – understanding barriers to learning and how to overcome them) that the teacher has of ***how to teach*** a subject (which informs the cycle of planning, teaching, marking and assessment) with a deep knowledge of the curriculum subject content (the national curriculum, the nature of science, key concepts within science subject knowledge and scientific misconceptions).

How does that nature of science, therefore, translate to teaching science in the primary classroom?

Figure 1.1 A mind map produced by a student teacher (non-science specialist) at the beginning of the Primary PGCE year

Figure 1.2 PCK (Pedagogical Content Knowledge; Shulman 1986) adapted by McCrory, A. (2017) to reflect the teaching, learning and assessment of science in primary schools in England and Wales

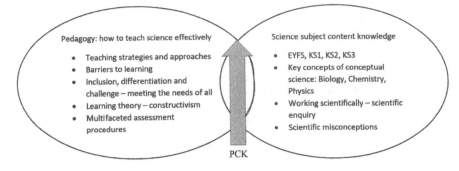

Pedagogy: how to teach science effectively

- Teaching strategies and approaches
- Barriers to learning
- Inclusion, differentiation and challenge – meeting the needs of all
- Learning theory – constructivism
- Multifaceted assessment procedures

Science subject content knowledge

- EYFS, KS1, KS2, KS3
- Key concepts of conceptual science: Biology, Chemistry, Physics
- Working scientifically – scientific enquiry
- Scientific misconceptions

PCK

Science is a never-ending journey of discovery by the curious and amassing of knowledge about the world – it is a collaborative endeavour!

Science is an ongoing process of discovery which informs an ever-growing body of knowledge; '*A scientist is someone who seeks, by systematic investigation, to understand experienced reality*' (Leroi 2014: 39).

In a letter to Robert Hooke (1676), Newton – who is without doubt considered one of the most influential scientists in history – famously quoted that, '*If I have seen further, it is by standing on the shoulder of giants!*'; scientists build on the foundations provided by the scientists who came before them and children need to understand this if we want them to understand that science is a human endeavour that anyone from any walk of life can contribute to and be successful in. Teaching this to children is now included in the KS2 curriculum for science; for example, when learning about Earth and Space, non-statutory guidance suggests that students should find out about how ideas about the solar system have developed over time by understanding why the geocentric model of the solar system was replaced by the heliocentric model by considering the work of Ptolemy, Copernicus and Galileo – evidence-informed!

Figure 1.3 The stimulus given to year 5 children to research and investigate the Geocentric and Heliocentric Models

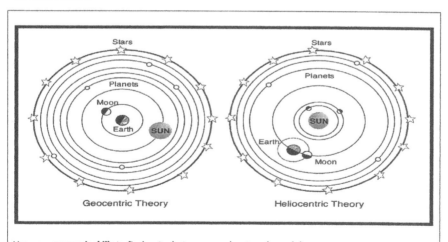

Use your **research skills** to find out what you can about each model.
Can you **explain** the differences between the two models?
How was **scientific evidence** used to support each model?
Use **scientific language** in your work!
What do you need to find out more about?

Figure 1.4 An example of a year 5 child's response to the challenge in Figure 1.3

Geocentric

Claudius Ptolemy (AD 100-170)
- Greek writer
- mathematician,
  astronomer

Geocentric Model =
a description of the Universe
with the sun at the centre

Evidence - Direct observation
- When looking at the sky, the
  sun appears to move around
  the Earth once a day.
- When standing on the Earth,
  it does not feel like it's
  moving.
- Ptolemy used astronomical
  observations by astronomers
  who came before him and
  his own observations to
  create his geometric model
  (800 years of observations).

Heliocentric

Galileo Galilei (1564-1642)
- Italian polymath
- astronomer, physicist
  mathematician

Heliocentric Model =
a description of the Universe
with the Earth at the centre.

Evidence - Observation
using a Telescope.
- heliocentric model first
  proposed by Copernicus -
  using a mathematical model.
- Kepler, expanded the model
  to include elliptical orbits.
- Galileo Galilei - observations
  of the Sun, Moon, Saturn and
  Jupiter (and its moons) - using
  a telescope, clear scientific
  evidence.

Need to know more about -
a) mathematical model, how does this work?
b) what is a celestial sphere?

Science allows us to link isolated facts into coherent and comprehensive understandings of the natural world; continually refining and expanding our knowledge of the universe and this requires collaboration. This, in turn, creates new questions for further investigation and so the cycle continues. An excellent example of this in the real-world being The Francis Crick Institute in London – an interdisciplinary biomedical research institute which offers a free programme of innovative and inclusive events and exhibitions designed to enlighten, inspire and entertain all ages about science. In the modern primary science classroom collaboration is key to progressing in scientific knowledge and understanding and process skills; collaborative learning is very important in improving scientific critical thinking skills.

The constructivist and social-constructivist learning perspectives have long been accepted as the dominant idea of learning in science (Skamp and Preston 2014). Learning in science being an active process where children make sense of the world around them by linking new conceptual knowledge to their existing frameworks ensuring that ideas and concepts in science make sense to them – constructing their knowledge on the basis of what they already know; developing understanding via the notion of learning from the More Knowledgeable Other; where pupils work together to search for meaning, understanding and/or solutions (Vygotsky 1978) which provide just the right amount of challenge for those taking part – thus learning through communication and interaction with others.

It is important to understand this 'ongoing' process in science, and primary-aged children are encouraged to understand that scientific ideas change and develop over time and see themselves as scientists in the classroom, rather than disconnected from 'real-life' science; therefore, science needs to be embedded in issues that are meaningful to children, valued and taught regularly – the last point is particularly important; children cannot be expected to develop their process skills or conceptual understanding if science is not embedded in the curriculum and visited weekly: *'The best teachers of science look for ways to enable their leaners as scientists!'* (Cross and Board 2014: 17).

When Amanda first started teaching, she asked her year 6 pupils to draw what they thought a scientist looked like; unsurprisingly, most of the pictures drawn were of white men, with grey fuzzy hair in white lab coats. More recently, she asked some year 6 children to name a scientist and what they do/did, some obvious answers included Sir David Attenborough, Mary Anning and Marie Curie; however, the children also mentioned Steve Backshall (naturalist and presenter of 'The Deadly 60'); Professor Brian Cox (physicist and The Royal Society Professor for Public Engagement) and the most popular Tim Peake (British Astronaut who has recently returned from the European Space Station) – some did also mention fictional characters such as Sheldon Cooper from the *Big Bang Theory*, a popular American show where science is revered and shown to be 'very cool'; Jane Foster a physicist from *Thor* (Marvel Films) and even Sandy Cheeks, a gifted inventor on *SpongeBob SquarePants*; demonstrating how science and scientists are becoming more visible to our children which can only be positive if we want to inspire our children to see themselves as future scientists. Pointedly, women still seem absent from the list, which certainly does not reflect our rich culture and ethnicity, more work clearly needs to be done to ensure children see themselves represented via the media.

Ofsted recognizes that the most effective science teachers make it a priority to *'first maintain curiosity'* (Ofsted 2013a: 4) in their pupils and if this is adopted as a key principle in the teaching of science via working scientifically then this will be fruitful in a number of ways:

- It will foster an enthusiasm and love for science while also promoting the notion of scholarship in the National Curriculum – this is the idea that teachers should be fostering a love of lifelong learning.

- It will combat the stereotypical image of a scientist which more often than not still, even today, predominantly involves a white man, in a lab coat, working alone in a laboratory strictly following the rules of an inflexible scientific method until he makes a discovery – no collaboration, no communication and no diversity. At some point in history, science has largely been the domain of white males but this is no longer the case and children need to understand that diversity is not only now the norm, but also facilitates specialization – the notion that different scientists who specialize in different areas within a field can indeed tackle the same topic from different angles resulting in a deeper understanding of the topic. This is important for children in the primary school to understand if we want them to see themselves as future innovators and scientists and if we want them to make links between science and other areas of the curriculum; for example, maths or music taking an in-depth, relational view of science rather than understanding scientific concepts in an isolated or procedural way.

- It will challenge, '*the entrenched viewpoints which depicts science as boring or just too difficult*' (CBI 2015: 3) so that primary-aged children are not switched off to science by the age of 11.

- Thereby enabling pupils to fulfil their potential; the message needs to be clear – STEM graduates are highly sought after in the workplace and a STEM qualification opens rather than closes doors.

Science has changed our lives and is vital for future economic growth!

We agree wholeheartedly with the national curriculum for science which states, '*A high-quality science education provides the foundations of understanding the world ... science has changed our lives and is vital to the world's future prosperity*' (DfE 2013: 3); it is essential that children understand this. Science generates knowledge which is reliable and which can be utilized to advance and develop new technologies which, when used responsibly, have the power to change people's lives!

Let us take 'Blade-runner' Richard Whitehead, the British athlete, as an example (Figure 1.5). Richard is a runner with prosthetic legs due to a double through-knee congenital amputation (born without a limb or limbs); he is also the world record

Figure 1.5 Richard Whitehead, British athlete

holder of the half-marathon for athletes with a double amputation. Without the special carbon-fibre-reinforced polymer prosthetics which were developed by Van Phillips, a medical engineer, what would Richard's life be like?

This invention has enabled Richard to surpass his goals. The message is as follows: life need not have limits; it is science which has delivered for Richard. The National Curriculum (2013) states that children need to understand the importance that science holds in their everyday lives and people in general; it also recognizes that children are interested in the world around them; they are naturally inquisitive and in the case of the 'Blade-runner' would be curious to know what his 'blades' are made of; how they work; whether or not they are comfortable; how they have improved his life.

'*The social and economic implications of science are important and should be taught within the wider school curriculum*' (DfE 2013: 3); for example, by giving children the opportunity to study the properties of materials and why they are suitable for particular purposes; and in this example, the creative uses for everyday materials, teachers are using different contexts to maximize their pupils' engagement with and motivation to study science. Examining science in this way also gives children a platform to discuss social issues relating to science which they might be experiencing from home; issues which are personal to them; for example, children now study inheritance in KS2.

Figure 1.6 How this became a platform for one child to discuss her own experiences of sickle-cell anaemia

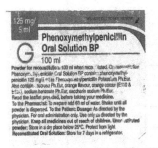

I have to take penicillin because I have Sickle Cell (a blood disorder) and this is what penicillin I have to take. I also have Thalasemia so I also have to take Folic Acid. I couldn't get the name of it, but I did try. My mum has Thalasemia and my dad has Sickle cell, so I have both (Sickle cell and Thalasemia trate). It is very hard for me to survive because if I get too cold, I could have a crysis and possibly die. I have had one before in my back and I was in hospital for eight days.

Science connects us, globally!

Science is a global human endeavour which is exciting! It is embedded in a global scientific community where scientists are motivated by solving problems, making new discoveries and conceiving new inventions in order to improve our daily lives and expand the collective knowledge of science. When Amanda was a child, she wrote to her pen pal in Malaysia – now, children can use Skype via computers, laptops, tablets and smart phones – how times have changed!

Scientists are creative, passionate people who are naturally curious – learning something new and being surprised by science is a compelling motivator. There is a unique pleasure in finding things out. Non-statutory guidance suggests that pupils find out about innovators, engineers and scientists when learning about different areas of science, for example, when identifying and discussing the uses of everyday materials KS1 pupils are encouraged to find out how John Dunlop developed a useful, new material (DfE 2013: 12); or children in upper KS2 studying life cycles of different animal groups might very well find out about the work of naturalists such as David Attenborough (DfE 2013: 27). Examining science as a global phenomenon enables primary teachers to make links across the primary curriculum.

Scientific literacy – the ability to be scientifically literate is more pertinent than ever!

There is a vast literature pertaining to the definition of scientific literacy and thus there is no agreed consensus in the scientific world on the definition of this (Millar 2007; Hodson 2008). For the readers of this book, we take the view that as we live in a world which is increasingly influenced by science and technology; for example, for the better – cancer treatments, and for the worse – the use of nuclear power as a weapon; therefore, decisions, relating to a wide range of issues made by individuals, need more than ever to be based in an understanding of scientific knowledge (scientific terminology and concepts, scientific enquiry and practice) and an understanding of the interactions between science technology and society. Thus, scientific literacy can be defined as the knowledge and understanding of scientific concepts and processes required to make informed personal decisions, and partake in political and cultural affairs. These skills do not start at secondary school!

The Government's Science and Learning Expert Group (2010) emphasized, '*The demand to make the curriculum more engaging and related to real-life contexts, as well as the desire to improve the scientific literacy of all young people.*' As educators, it is our responsibility to ensure that the children in our care – citizens of the future – develop their knowledge and understanding about science-related situations and this starts at a young age, at primary school age. From our own teaching and research experience, we can categorically state that children care passionately and want to know more about the world in which they live; they are highly motivated by and interested in contemporary issues, many of which have a scientific basis (Claire and Holden 2007; Sadler 2011).

Bruner (1966) argued the notion of a spiral curriculum and stated that any subject can be taught in some intellectually honest form to any child at any stage of development as long as their cognitive capabilities are taken into account. The national curriculum for science reflects his ideology. Bruner's position was that children need to learn the underlying principles of different concepts rather than simply memorize facts; noting that when children engage in discovery learning they construct knowledge internally and rely on this internal cognitive structures to bring meaning to learning experiences. Therefore, he championed learning through enquiry – as does the national curriculum for science with its emphasis on primary school children 'working scientifically' – with the goal being that children construct and grasp basic ideas in conceptual science. As children develop and mature, they revisit earlier learnt ideas, expanding on them until they are able to see how individual ideas relate to one another; seeing ideas as relational rather than isolated and procedural thus understanding scientific concepts in more depth.

Now let us turn to the second question, does your understanding of the nature of science differ to your understanding of primary science – what does primary science teaching look like to you?

This is an important question to consider because, often, this is where the aims and outcomes of science education can become muddied. Chapters 3 and 4 discuss in depth how facilitators of science education can promote children's engagement in and enjoyment of science in the primary classroom but here we turn to the question of learning and understanding conceptual science, alongside developing scientific process skills. Generally, primary-aged children enjoy the practical side of science; however, it has also been recognized that more needs to be done to improve its effectiveness in developing conceptual understanding of science (Abrahams and Reiss 2012). The inexperienced or ineffectual teacher can focus too much on children having 'fun via exploration' – yes, fun is important in order to engage children in scientific learning – exploration and enquiry are crucial in developing process skills; however, it is important to remember that without the conceptual learning, then the outcomes of enquiry will be just that – fun, without children progressing in their conceptual understanding of science. Teachers, school leaders and governors need to be clear on the *aims of primary science education and what is achievable*; high expectations of outcomes in science education for **all** children in primary schools is not simply an expectation from the government but what each and every child *deserves!* Chapter 8 discusses inclusion and high expectations for all in more depth.

Therefore, what does it mean to be scientific in the primary classroom?

If you cannot explain it simply, then you do not understand it! (Einstein)

Science in the primary schools focuses on biology, chemistry and physics – via these disciplines scientific knowledge and conceptual understanding is taught and developed. Scientific enquiry – referred to in the national curriculum for science as 'working scientifically' – is an essential tool for children to ask and answer scientific questions about the world around them. Understanding the nature, processes and methods of science is an important aim of science education in the primary school:

● *While it is important that pupils make progress, it is also vitally important that they develop secure understanding of each key block of knowledge and concepts in order to progress to the next stage. Insecure, superficial understanding will not allow genuine progression: pupils may struggle at key points of transition (such as between primary and secondary school), build up serious misconceptions, and/or have significant difficulties in understanding higher-order content.*

- *Pupils should be able to describe associated processes and key characteristics in common language, but they should also be familiar with, and use, technical terminology accurately and precisely.*

- *They should build up an extended specialist vocabulary. They should also apply their mathematical knowledge to their understanding of science, including collecting, presenting and analysing data.*

- *The social and economic implications of science are important but, generally, they are taught most appropriately within the wider school curriculum: teachers will wish to use different contexts to maximise their pupils' engagement with and motivation to study science.* (DfE 2013: 3)

In addition, working scientifically specifies the understanding of the nature, processes and methods of science for each year group and should be embedded within the content of biology, chemistry and physics, focusing on the key features of scientific enquiry, so that pupils learn to use a variety of approaches to answer relevant scientific questions. These types of scientific enquiry should include:

- *Observing over time;*
- *pattern seeking;*
- *identifying,*
- *classifying and grouping;*
- *comparative and fair testing (controlled investigations); and researching using secondary sources*

Pupils should seek answers to questions through collecting, analysing and presenting data (DfE 2013: 3).

Figure 1.7 gives examples of how some of these priorities have been achieved in one primary school setting.

'"Working scientifically" will be developed further at key stages 3 and 4, once pupils have built up sufficient understanding of science to engage meaningfully in more sophisticated discussion of experimental design and control' (DfE 2013: 4). Scientific process skills need to be developed as they are the bedrock for children to be able to understand conceptual science; as well as engage in and enjoy science. The Wellcome Trust (2013) note that children start to *develop perceptions about whether science is for them towards the end of primary school*' (2013: 4) and it is therefore imperative that all, not some, primary school children experience exciting and inspiring science that reinforces their understanding of the nature of science. However, let us now take a closer look at what this means in key stage 1, lower and upper key stage 2.

Figure 1.7 A display board reflecting the science work undertaken across a primary school – with thanks to Aveley Primary School, Essex

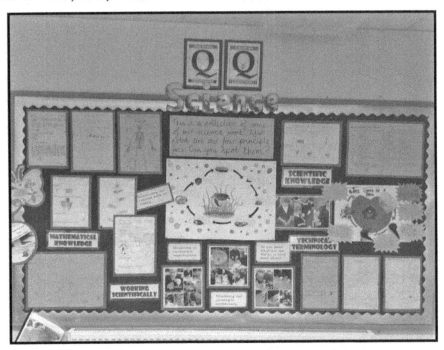

Working scientifically in key stage 1

The national curriculum for England programme of study (2013) states that the principal focus of science teaching in key stage 1 is as follows:

- *To enable pupils to experience and **observe phenomena**, looking more closely at the natural and humanly-constructed world around them.*

- *They **should be encouraged to be curious and ask questions** about what they notice.*

- *They should **be helped to develop their understanding of scientific ideas** by using different types of scientific enquiry to answer their own questions, including observing changes over a period of time, noticing patterns, grouping and classifying things, carrying out simple comparative tests, and finding things out using secondary sources of information.*

- *They should **begin to use simple scientific language** to talk about what they have found out and communicate their ideas to a range of audiences in a variety of ways. Most of the learning about science should be done through* *the use of **first-hand practical experiences,** but there should also be some use of appropriate secondary sources, such as books, photographs and videos.*

- *Working scientifically must always be taught through and clearly related to the teaching of **substantive science content** in the programme of study.*

- *Pupils should **read and spell scientific vocabulary** at a level consistent with their increasing word reading and spelling knowledge at key stage 1.*
  (DfE 2013: 5)

Pause for thought – *Insects*

- Look at the following figures, 1.8 and 1.9; what do you deduce that the year 2 child knows about ants?

Figure 1.8 A year 2 child's observational drawing of an ant

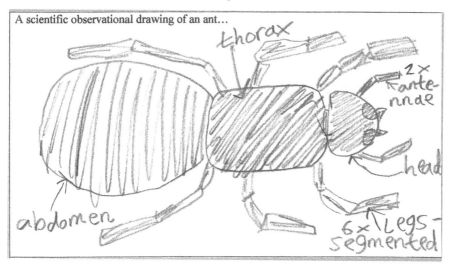

Figure 1.9 A year 2 child's work on the topic of insects; observational drawing and pattern seeking

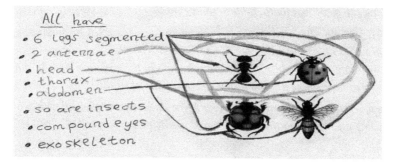

Our reflections about Figure 1.8 and 1.9 are as follows:

- The child can use, and spell correctly, scientific vocabulary to label an ant and to find similarities (patterns) about insects; effectively this child can scientifically name the features of an insect.

- The observational drawing (process skill) demonstrates attention to detail; body parts are correctly labelled and proportional; segmented legs are attempted (although not always successfully) and joined to the thorax, not the thorax and the abdomen which is a common misconception; therefore, the observational drawing has enabled the child to be much more scientifically accurate.

- Compound eyes and mandibles are included but not labelled; interestingly, compound eyes and an exoskeleton are included in Figure 1.8. When assessing this, we would most likely ask the child to demonstrate or explain, in their own way, the meaning of an exoskeleton and compound eyes. To extend the child further, we might ask them to create their own insect using the scientific features they have identified when seeking patterns. Indeed, we might ask the child to think about whether or not all insects have wings (and why, why not) and explain their reasoning again either orally, pictorially or in writing.

Working scientifically in lower key stage 2

The national curriculum for England programme of study states that the principal focus of science teaching in lower key stage 2 is as follows:

- *To enable pupils to **broaden their scientific view** of the world around them. They should do this through exploring, talking about, testing and developing ideas about everyday phenomena and the **relationships** between living things and familiar environments, and **by beginning to develop their ideas about functions, relationships and interactions.***

- *They **should ask their own questions** about what they observe and **make some decisions** about which types of scientific enquiry are likely to be the best ways of answering them, including observing changes over time, noticing patterns, grouping and classifying things, carrying out simple comparative and fair tests and finding things out using secondary sources of information.*

- ***They should draw simple conclusions and use some scientific language**, first, to talk about and, later, to write about what they have found out. 'Working scientifically' must always be taught through and clearly related to substantive science content in the programme of study.*

- *Pupils should read and spell scientific vocabulary correctly and with confidence, using their growing word reading and spelling knowledge.* (DfE 2013: 13)

> ## Pause for thought – *Teeth*
>
> - What do you know about teeth?
> - What have you deduced that the year 4 child knows scientifically about teeth in Figure 1.10.
> - What does his work reveal about any gaps in his knowledge or his alternative ideas of scientific misconceptions?
> - What aspects of scientific enquiry does the child suggest?

Our reflections on Figure 1.10 are as follows:

- The child has been given the opportunity to think about the subject and ask any questions about it which interest him, as well as consider the types of enquiry he could do to find the answers.

- Questions asked are declarative, related closely to the focus – teeth and demonstrate how the child is asking exploratory questions (evidence of higher-order thinking skills) to extend the knowledge that he already has (e.g. knows that sugar is bad for teeth but not why; knows that animals have teeth [and includes humans as animals, clear evidence of understanding a key concept in biology] but would like to know which animal has the strongest teeth).

- Ideas for finding answers to the questions include research, interviews and observations (enquiry skills).

- The question regarding the wisdom teeth could be explored further to see if there is an underlying misconception about when wisdom teeth grow; the question regarding bones and teeth would need further clarification – he is

Figure 1.10 A year 4 child's questions about teeth and ideas on how to find out the answers

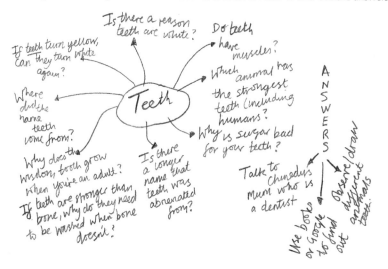

trying to make a connection between his scientific knowledge of bones and teeth but we would ask the child to explain further what he means by this question via a discussion where we could then scaffold his thinking.

Working scientifically in upper key stage 2

The national curriculum for England programme of study states that the principal focus of science teaching in lower key stage 2 is as follows:

- *To enable pupils to develop a **deeper understanding** of a wide range of scientific ideas. They should do this through exploring and talking about their ideas; asking their own questions about scientific phenomena; and analysing functions, relationships and interactions more systematically.*

- *At upper key stage 2, they should encounter **more abstract ideas** and begin to recognise how these ideas help them to understand and predict how the world operates.*

- *They should also begin to recognise that **scientific ideas change and develop** over time.*

- *They should **select the most appropriate ways to answer science questions using different types of scientific enquiry**, including observing changes over different periods of time, noticing patterns, grouping and classifying things, carrying out comparative and fair tests and finding things out using a wide range of secondary sources of information.*

- *Pupils should **draw conclusions based on their data and observations**, use evidence to justify their ideas, and use their scientific knowledge and understanding to explain their findings.*

- *'Working and thinking scientifically' must always be taught through and clearly related to **substantive science content** in the programme of study.*

- *Pupils should read, spell and pronounce scientific vocabulary correctly.*
  (DfE 2013: 24)

Pause for thought – *Scientific enquiry*

What evidence is there in the year 6 child's work (Figure 1.11) of her:

a) Using evidence to explain her findings?

b) Using scientific knowledge and understanding to explain her findings?

Figure 1.11 A year 6 child drawing her conclusions based on data, observations and evidence as well as using her scientific knowledge and understanding

Q – Prove light travels in straight lines.

There are some really easy ways to observe and prove that light travels in straight lines.

a projector   using a torch in the dark

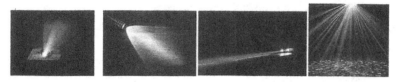

headlights on a car at night cool strobe lights

My investigation:

I put three peces of card – all the same size and the same thickness – with a hole in the middle,

the size of a ten pence piece – and then I first arranged them in a uneven line.

The light stops and cannot travel through all three cards.

I repeated my investigation but this time I put the cards in a straight line.

The light is able to travel through all three cards because it is travelling in a straight line.

Our reflections on Figure 1.11 are as follows, the child has:

- Used ICT to investigate how light travels in a straight line
- Then conducted her own investigation to prove how light travels in a straight line
- Used scientific vocabulary correctly and confidently
- Been given the freedom to investigate and present her scientific thinking in a creative way

Working scientifically and scientific enquiry will be examined in more depth in chapters 3, 4, 5 and 8.

How can the teaching of science in the primary school contribute to a child's whole education?

We have already discussed, to some degree, the social, cultural, economic and ethical advantages children will benefit from by studying science; these benefits are transferable across the curriculum. Therefore, understanding how science teaching can positively impact on the outcomes of learning across the curriculum is imperative. When teaching, making links between what is being learnt and the 'bigger picture' while drawing attention to patterns in and between different areas of the curriculum is what primary teachers do very well. For example, the analysis skills that children learn while engaging in science are transferable to other areas of the curriculum, in particular playing a strong role in English, maths, geography and history; embedding these skills across the curriculum can only benefit our children in the long run.

This links clearly to the spiral curriculum but also to the aims of science education in general which require children to understand and make links between the big ideas of science education (Harlen 2010); for example, applications of science often have ethical, social, economic and political implications. This will hopefully help teachers feel empowered to deliver a balanced and fair curriculum; links to the wider curriculum will be discussed in more depth throughout this book.

Science and developing resilience – why taking risks and making mistakes is crucial when learning!

'We all live under the same sky, but don't all have the same horizon' – how a Growth Mindset can help us reach our potential.

Do you think that learning science is only for those who have the intelligence or a natural aptitude for the subject? If you do, the following will challenge your thinking.

World renowned psychologist Carol Dweck (Stanford University) has been researching and collecting data about people's beliefs regarding how they learn for many years. Her ground-breaking work argues that there are two differing mindsets – a 'growth or fixed mindset' (2006, 2017) – which leads to different learning behaviours and therefore has the potential to impact positively or negatively on the learning outcomes of the children we teach. People with a fixed mindset believe that their intelligence and basic abilities are fixed traits that cannot be changed; therefore, time is spent documenting their intelligence rather than developing it. There is also the belief that talent alone – without effort – is enough to succeed. Contrary to this, people with a growth mindset believe that intelligence is not fixed and that they can learn and improve through dedication and hard work; talent and intelligence is simply the starting point. Dweck argues that teaching a growth mindset in the classroom creates motivation and productivity while creating a love of learning and a resilience that is essential for children to achieve. In relation to science in particular, Dweck (1999, 2008) also argues:

a) *that mindsets can predict science achievement over time;*

b) *that mindsets can contribute to achievement discrepancies for women and minorities;*

c) *interventions that change mindsets from fixed to growth can boost achievement and reduce discrepancies in science achievement;*

d) *that educators play a key role in shaping students' mindsets* (2008: 2).

Developing a 'growth mindset' takes time and involves a shift in a child's mindset from fearing mistakes to learning from them. Learning science is often about taking risks; in order to do this, children must be willing to fail. This occurs naturally in the EYFS and therefore teachers need to ask themselves why it is that by KS2 some children are afraid to fail? Therefore, the ethos in your classroom must be one which takes risks, celebrates mistakes, promotes a growth mindset (achievement in science is possible for all) and sees these as an opportunity to learn and improve.

Figure 1.12 Using Einstein to reflect on making mistakes

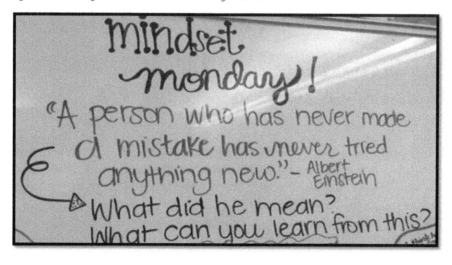

Figure 1.13 Conversations between children and teachers which exemplify a 'growth mindset'

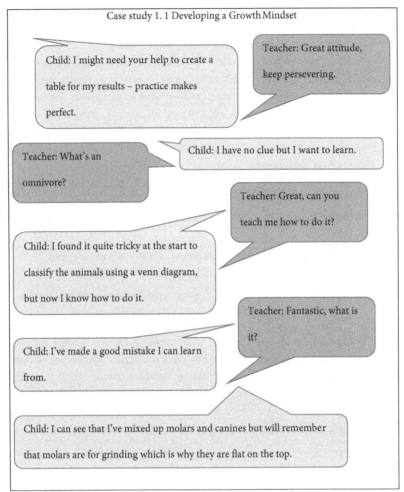

Case study 1. 1 Developing a Growth Mindset

Child: I might need your help to create a table for my results – practice makes perfect.

Teacher: Great attitude, keep persevering.

Teacher: What's an omnivore?

Child: I have no clue but I want to learn.

Teacher: Great, can you teach me how to do it?

Child: I found it quite tricky at the start to classify the animals using a venn diagram, but now I know how to do it.

Teacher: Fantastic, what is it?

Child: I've made a good mistake I can learn from.

Child: I can see that I've mixed up molars and canines but will remember that molars are for grinding which is why they are flat on the top.

Motivation to learn and high expectations for all!

Collins (2015) argues that because of strides in neuro-educational research, the fastest-growing area of research in education, learning takes place at a cellular level – it is a process which takes place over time, connecting neurons and changing the way brain cells communicate; creating new synapses and connections which changes the way your brain is organized.

The first stage in learning is motivation and persistence is a required state for most learning – children need to practise, repeat, try again and practise. Exploration increases creativity and brain plasticity which helps children become open to new ideas and be more creative in their own ideas; all strong arguments for teaching science, especially scientific enquiry, regularly. When children are curious, dopamine is released in the brain which may act as a reward in itself but more importantly this is implicated in a goal-directed behaviour (Collins 2015). As we know, facilitating and promoting curiosity in science education is integral to the new curriculum (Ofsted 2013).

Active processing includes relating new experiences and learning to previous experiences and real-life events and this is an important part of the brain-based approach to learning: situated learning, authentic contexts, the importance of prior learning and engagement. This is closely related to 'mental processing' as described by constructionist theorists (Piaget 1972; Perry 1999), the notion that all new learning builds upon a foundation of what has gone before and the relating of new information to old engages and motivates children to learn.

High expectations for all! Complex learning is enhanced by challenge – if teaching is pitched too low then learners will be under stimulated; equally poor is pitching work at the precise level of the learning as this will result in little learning as children are in their comfort zone. Therefore, providing children with opportunities to be challenged but not pitched so high that the work is impossible encourages learners to become engaged; this strongly links with Vygotsky's argument of the 'Zone of Proximal Development' (1978) pitching work to challenge all children is a skill that every teacher needs to hone, regardless of the subject being taught. Providing challenge for all children, especially the brightest, in science requires attention by schools especially in the provision of scientific enquiry (Ofsted 2013; Wellcome 2013); inclusion and challenge for all is discussed in more depth in Chapter 8.

Summary

- Science endeavours to understand the world and beyond.
- Science has changed our lives and children need to understand the importance of this.
- Science is a never-ending journey of discovery – it is not static.
- Scientific ideas are subject to change but build on the ideas of scientists that have come before and children need to understand this.
- Science is a global, human endeavour which celebrates diversity.
- Science is not only for those who are seen as having the intelligence or aptitude for it; science is for everyone and children need to understand this if we are to ensure that they see that science is for them – that a career in science is achievable for anyone.
- In effect, when learning science in primary schools, children are learning about the nature of science.

- Constructivism and social-constructivism is at the heart of learning science.
- In primary science, process skills must be developed alongside conceptual scientific knowledge and understanding; children achieve this by 'working scientifically'.
- It is our responsibility as science educators to ensure that our children become scientifically literate adults.
- Science contributes in many ways to a child's whole education; cross-curricular links should be encouraged.

Recommended reading

Dunne, M. and Peacock, A. (2015). *Primary Science – A Guide to Teaching Practice*, 2nd ed. Sage.

Harlen, W. ed. (2010). *Principles and Big Ideas of Science Education*, Association for Science Education, Hatfield.

Harlen, W. (2011). *The ASE Guide to Primary Science Education*. ASE.

Roden, J. and Archer, J. (2014). *Primary Science for Trainee Teachers*. Learning Matters.

Russell, T. and McGuigan, L. (2016). *Exploring Science with Young Children*. Sage.

Chapter 2
Current Developments in Primary Science

You can do the best research and be making the strongest intellectual argument, but if readers don't get past the third paragraph, you've wasted your energy and valuable ink.

Carl Hiessan – novelist

Chapter objectives

By the end of this chapter you will have developed an understanding of:

- Why using evidence-informed research to underpin your provision of science education can only improve your pedagogical content knowledge (PCK) [Shulman 1986; 2015]) as discussed in Chapter 1;

- The current state of primary science – the status and provision of science education in primary schools;

- What recent and relevant research in science education has to say about primary science; what works – the positives of primary science; and the challenges – what teachers and schools need to consider in their provision for science.

Introduction

Being mindful of the audience of this book, we feel it important to highlight both the current strengths and challenges of primary science provision in schools in England and Wales so that trainee teachers are aware of what effective provision of science is. It is important to us as science educators that the readers of this book are equipped with the knowledge and understanding of what good practice in primary science teaching is so that if, or indeed when, challenges are encountered in school, trainee teachers (or indeed any reader of this book) are able to critically reflect on and, where necessary, challenge what they experience. This is something we would expect our student trainee teachers at UCL Institute of Education (IOE) to do. We are not interested in promoting anything less than the highest quality provision of science in primary schools; unfortunately, the reality is that this does not, yet, exist in every primary school in England and Wales. Therefore, this chapter discusses the current status of science in primary schools as a core subject; this is important because science is a core subject – although often not treated as such – and there are statutory requirements to adhere to. Followed by an examination of children's and teachers' attitudes to science, this knowledge being powerful and often underestimated. Reflections on the strengths and weaknesses of provision in primary science are then illuminated.

The quote at the start of this chapter, without doubt, resonates with many – does it to you? Just as science educationists – and the government – would argue that professionals in schools have a responsibility to keep themselves informed of relevant developments within the field of science education; teachers, we are sure, would argue that science education researchers have a responsibility to make effective outcomes of research easily accessible and easy to implement in the classroom. Of course, both parties are correct – although this is not always recognized, or understood by all! It is indisputable that research is needed to make progress (Allen 2016) and if it is to have an impact in the classroom and not simply be theoretical, then it needs to be tested and developed in the classroom so that the outcomes that are effective have wide reaching advantages and gains. There should be, to borrow an apt biological term, a symbiotic relationship between the two; ultimately, a marriage which can only benefit all who take part.

Those involved in providing science education for children in primary schools, we would argue, are open and welcome to, being guided by not simply the latest research, but research with is proven to be successful in the classroom. This is unmistakeably needed when we understand that only 3 per cent of primary school teachers in England and Wales are in possession of an undergraduate degree in science (Royal Society 2010). It is no secret that the work–life balance of teachers is capricious – so where do teachers find the time to read the latest research because although they recognize the importance of using research to inform their teaching; often lack of time and support from senior leaders for teachers to achieve this is wanting (Education Endowment Foundation 2016).

This is not the only barrier to teachers reading recent and relevant research to inform their practice. There is also the issue of access – although the internet is a relatively free resource, journal articles and books are not; so, where do teachers start among the sea of journals and research papers? How do they know what works well and, perhaps more importantly, what challenges they need to recognize and overcome when providing science education for the children they teach because this is not always obvious, especially to the non-specialist?

Figure 2.1 The modern-day primary classroom practitioner. Does this image seem familiar to you?

What is the current state of primary science?

Will science in primary schools ever be a core subject? (Farrow 2006: 311)

In 1989, although there was a considerable amount of debate regarding the introduction of a National Curriculum and the statutory content included; science educationists applauded its introduction as the first steps towards the statutory entitlement *of all pupils* to science education; for all too often, science provision in schools was inconsistent, with falling standards an increasing concern (House of Commons: Children, Schools and Families Committee 2009). Science, along with English and maths, was given the status of a 'core subject' which is specified at each key stage through detailed programmes of study. Would this ensure that the status of science finally matched that of English and maths? In 2006, Steve Farrow's research project – designed to investigate the impact of the National Curriculum, in particular the provision of science, in schools – set out to measure the 'rhetoric against the reality' (2006: 311).

Dishearteningly, Farrow (2006) found a vast variation in the time devoted to science teaching reported in successive surveys by fourth year B.Ed. students. Evidence suggested that time devoted to science teaching reflected around one third of the teaching of maths and English. In addition, evidence provided by PGCE students argued that the teaching of science had become – as far as classroom practitioners were concerned – de facto, a foundation subject, where, in some schools, science was only included in time allocated to topic work. Perhaps the most demoralizing for Farrow was the perception held by the majority of teachers, who took part in the survey, that maths and English should take precedence over science. That was ten years ago, since then, the National Curriculum has been reformed (2013); therefore, how has the climate of teaching science in the primary school changed? Take a moment now, to think honestly about the following pause for thought before reading on!

Pause for thought – *Pre-Service Teachers*

- What science learning have you observed in schools?
- What does this science teaching look like?
- Is there a disparity between what you see and what you are being taught at university or at school if you are on a school-based route (including your readings in the field of science education) or do you think you are seeing good practice in the provision of science?
- How is it taught and how frequently?
- What does this tell you about the status of science in the schools you have visited?
- How confident are you in your science subject knowledge?

Pause for thought – *Teachers, Science Coordinators, SLT*

- How often do you teach science?
- How often are you observed or observe others teaching science?
- When observing science, how confident are you in understanding the conceptual science and process skills?
- What CPD provision is provided for science in your school?
- How would you describe the status of science in your school?
- How confident do you feel assessing science, especially Evolution and process skills?
- How often is progress and attainment in science monitored?
- How confident are you in your science teaching pedagogy including subject knowledge?
- What are the positives and what are the challenges for you in teaching or organizing provision for science?
- Why do you think does or does not have the same status as the other core subjects? What role do you play in raising its status in your school?

Recent findings regarding the teaching of science in primary schools – provision for science education in primary schools; status

In September 2015, a Wellcome Trust review examined the extent to which Ofsted reports about English schools mention science. They were interested in examining this, given concerns that science has been losing its status in many primary schools in recent years (Ofsted 2013); and the authority and influence that Ofsted has on the behaviour of schools with its role in verifying teaching and learning of a broad and balanced curriculum. Is the provision of science in primary schools a priority for Ofsted? Results were not surprising to those of us in the world of primary science education but perhaps, in light of your reflections and school experience, *are they to you?*

A preliminary review of Ofsted's full inspection reports from 770 primary schools found that 93 per cent of reports *did not mention science at all*. This prompted a more thorough examination of recent reports using a sample of 100 schools in 2014; 73 per cent of primary school inspection reports *did not mention science* – 100 per cent mentioned maths and English. In comparison, in Northern Ireland 90 per cent of primary school reports did not mention science; 80 per cent in Scotland – with only Wales bucking this trend; 100 per cent of primary school reports undertaken in Wales mentioned science. As we know, the Department for Education's (DfE) stance is that 'science is a compulsory subject in schools from 5–16'; therefore, how do Ofsted explain their lack of focus on the provision for science when inspecting primary schools and the conflicting message that this sends to those responsible for *science provision in primary schools?*

Good intentions?

When the DfE abolished science SATs testing in 2009, in favour of teacher assessment, it was recognized that this move, in part, was a response to alleviate the pressures on curriculum time and to allow children to develop an enthusiasm for science. Note that SATs testing for English and maths remained and continued to be published in league tables along with the introduction of Level 6 testing in 2012 – although these have since been abandoned – to cater for children who were categorized as more able in English and maths (the top 2 per cent in the country, whose work in class reflected the standard expected of a 14-year-old). Clearly enthusiasm for English and maths was not an issue – neither was the pressure on the curriculum, teachers or pupils in the eyes of the Government!

The decision to abolish science SATs backfired hugely and in itself devalued the status of science; some schools – pressured by the expectations of attainment for English and maths; and the knowledge that English and maths would be the focus of inspections rather than science – took more and more of the curriculum to focus on these areas – not good news for science, or for all the other subjects in the primary curriculum. The impact of this was not lost on those working in science education. The Confederation of British Industry (CBI) director general John Cridland (2015: 3) noted that,

> Science education in primary schools is being squeezed out, with too many schools struggling to teach the recommended two hours per week

The NFER Teacher Voice Survey (Wellcome Trust 2016) found that of the 740 respondents to the survey; 48 per cent taught between 1 and 2 hours of science per week; 19 per cent taught 30 minutes to one hour – with a small percentage, 4 per cent, teaching less than 30 minutes per week. In addition to those surveyed, 24 per cent noted that they did not teach science every week. More recently, the 'State of the nation' report of UK primary science education (2017) found that on average 58 per cent of classes in primary schools are not receiving two hours of weekly science with 12 per cent of the schools surveyed (1,010 teachers and 902 science leaders) not delivering weekly science lessons to any year group – one then must ask the question of how schools who don't teach science weekly or for the recommended amount of time, expect the children they teach to make progress in their conceptual understanding of science alongside their process skills? While it is important to note that primary schools also deliver science via cross-curricular lessons with this being more likely in Reception and KS1 (CFE, 2017); we feel it also important to highlight that process skills cannot simply be honed, in an ad hoc fashion and this might well account for the findings by Oftsed (2011, 2013), who found that assessment for scientific enquiry was not well developed in some primary schools and that there was less planning for different needs in scientific enquiry than in knowledge and understanding. They argued that programmes of study of science education for all year groups should be balanced, providing opportunities for children to develop their knowledge and understanding of scientific concepts while developing their process skills; hence the changes to the national curriculum.

Cridland (2015) also maintained that over half of the teachers surveyed in the *Tomorrow's World* report stated that they believed that the teaching of science in primary schools has become less of a priority. Anecdotal evidence, from my PGCE students, concurs with this. At the start of the academic year, one of the main issues we find when setting science tasks for PGCE students to undertake during school placements is the issue of whether or not the school will be teaching science. The first task is to observe science lessons in different key stages, a small percentage (around 10 per cent) find that this is difficult or in some cases impossible to organize because their placement school is not teaching science during the term, in any year group!

Therefore, what is on the horizon?

However, a glimmer of hope emerged in May, 2016. Sir Michael Wilshaw – Ofsted's then Chief Inspector – and ultimately the representative of the 'professional body' best placed to challenge the climate of science teaching in schools, commented on the study of science in primary schools. He noted that the emphasis on English and mathematics in primary schools, although essential, should not be at the expense of other important subjects, such as science. He recognized that science, although a core compulsory subject, had become, in some schools the poor relation of the primary school curriculum; that there was lack of teaching expertise to support teachers in teaching science and that poor working arrangements with partner secondary schools meant that transitions and progression from KS2 to KS3 was ineffective.

Why suddenly the increased focus on primary science by Ofsted, especially if we take the Wellcome Trust's (2016) review of Ofsted reports as discussed earlier into consideration? We would like to say that this is in response to the science education community who, for a long time, have fervently and passionately voiced their concerns and recommendations; is it possible that this has played a part? In part, yes. The economic impact on the country by not producing scientists is well documented (Wellcome 2013; Cridland 2015). In addition, the answer lies perhaps with the government's concerns over the number of students taking science at GCSE – only 74 per cent of pupils took science to the GCSE level needed to qualify for the Baccalaureate (EBacc) in 2015 – the Government aims for the majority of pupils, who started secondary school in September 2015, to take the full suite of English EBacc subjects which includes science; therefore, the issue must be addressed.

Children's attitudes to science

Pause for thought

- In your opinion, how do you think children view science?
- Do you think there is a difference between how girls and boys view science?
- Do you think primary-aged pupils think differently about science from secondary-aged students?
- On the whole, do you think their attitude to learning about science and the world around them is positive or negative?

At heart, we are teachers – and as science educators nothing gives us more pleasure than engaging with children when they are learning science. We have never met a child who is not curious and does not want to investigate in science unless they have experienced the boredom on not being taught science effectively. We are now very fortunate because we can experience this on a much larger scale via our university students; we are very lucky indeed.

We know from research investigating children's attitudes to science that, in general, primary-aged pupils have very positive attitudes to practical science and that this tends to emerge from a young age (Murphy, Biggs and Russell 2005; Silver and Rushton 2008; Berland and Hammer 2012; Tunnicliffe 2015); they tend to leave primary school thinking positively about science. The 'State of the nation' report of UK primary science education (2017: 8) which surveyed 1,906 pupils (aged 7-11) found that 44 per cent of primary-aged pupils like science at school 'alot' (with 41 per cent liking science respectively); 93 per cent of pupils agreeing that 'they like to understand how things work', and 87 per cent finding science 'interesting'. Interestingly, 30 per cent of the pupils surveyed reported they would like a science-related job when they grow up although still future job choices were engendered; boys being more likely to want a job in engineering or a similar discipline; and girls more likely to want a job as a vet or a career in medicine. The collaborative, social constructivist approach to teaching and learning science does much to motivate and engage students in learning science and teachers who focus on including curiosity and creativity to promote scientific thinking and reasoning skills are in fact equipping learners with lifelong skills (Ofsted 2013: Ward and Roden 2016).

Barriers to learning and enjoying science for some children lie with the classroom teacher and his or her teaching pedagogy, as well as the learning environment. For some children, the learning of conceptual science is a challenge and science is hard to learn; 43 per cent of primary-aged children surveyed by the CFE (2017) endorse this view, they stated that they agreed with the statement that someone needs to be clever to do science. The scientific vocabulary, counter-intuitive concepts, abstract concepts, scientific misconceptions that have already formed, the over use of worksheets, use of disengaging teaching strategies or learning facts do nothing to engage children in science learning (Allen 2014; Loxley et al. 2013).

Teachers' attitudes to teaching science

Factors contributing to children's attitudes to learning science also include those of the class teacher. As a primary school science teacher, and most probably a non-science specialist (with only 3 per cent of primary school teachers holding a science degree), how you feel about teaching, and value, science will have a direct impact on how you teach it. In Chapter 1, we asked you to consider honestly, your thoughts and feelings about the nature of science; now we ask you to reflect on your attitude to teaching science. At the beginning of the PGCE year, we talk with our students about their attitude to be a science teacher. Very few tell us they hate it (although some do); often, we hear a mixture of the following:

Van Aalderman-Smeets and Van der Molen (2013) argue that one of the major challenges in science education is improving the attitudes of some primary teachers towards teaching science and they are not alone (Pell and Jarvis 2003; Sharp, Hopkin and Lewthwaite 2011; Farrow 2017). We see this as an important aim of what we do at UCL/IOE for our students; modelling good practice in science teaching, provoking critical thinking and reflection while providing plenty of support to aid our students' science subject knowledge, play an integral role in this – it is important to us that our students feel confident, enthusiastic and positive to teach science in the primary school and enabling our students to become this is at the heart of our role and who we are as science educators.

Figure 2.2 Student teachers' reflections on teaching primary science

Student teachers' reflections on teaching science in the primary classroom

- I love science – it's so creative, so much fun – finding out about how things work and making sense of the world. I can't wait to teach it, children just love science lessons and they're so much more interesting than literacy lessons.
- I don't mind science. I've had mixed experiences with it in the past but can see how much children enjoy it and I hope to be able to teach it well.
- I am so worried about teaching science; I find it a really hard subject to understand, especially physics, and there's so much I don't know. I worry how I will control the children to let them investigate.

When taken at face value, this provocative statement above regarding teachers' attitudes to teaching science is bound to invoke some negative reactions by hard working primary school teachers who already, too often, feel solely responsible for the outcomes of pupil progress, especially in today's accountability culture.

Teaching is a reflective process (Pollard 2014); recent findings from the NFER Teacher Voice Survey (Wellcome Trust 2016) echoes these concerns regarding teacher attitudes; with 17 per cent stating that they only sometimes enjoy teaching science. This is echoed by the findings of the CFE (2017); when asked about confidence to teach and assess primary science (10 per cent of teachers surveyed stated that they were not confident in this, with up to 18 per cent neither agreeing nor disagreeing with the statement of being confident in this). Barriers to teaching science for those who responded included a lack of time; curricula importance; lack of budget and resources; lack of subject knowledge and issues relating to setting up space of access to resources.

Van Aalderman-Smeets and Van der Molen's (2013) theoretical framework for the construct of primary teachers' attitudes towards science highlights three dimensions which contribute to a teacher's attitude towards teaching science – *cognitive, affective and perceived control.* I state them here so that you can reflect on these in relation to your own attitudes.

- *Cognition* – the first dimension refers to cognitive, subjective beliefs about teaching primary school science which includes perceived relevance and perceived difficulty (Ofsted 2013; CBI 2015;) that teachers attribute to the task of teaching science in primary schools (not to be confused with self-efficacy, a teacher's perception about the own capability in teaching) and gender-stereotypical beliefs about teaching science (teachers' perceptions or beliefs about differences between boys and girls, not actual differences between them), for example that girls are not interested in learning science (DCSF 2007).

- *Affective* – the second dimension encompasses the positive and negative subjective emotions a teacher might experience when teaching science; enjoyment and anxiety. These two affective components are not opposites; it is possible to enjoy teaching science but feel anxious about it. Analysing the causes of anxiety and addressing these is key to overcoming these issues (Pollard 2014).

- *Perceived control* – the third dimension is also subjective and refers to the amount of perceived control a teacher has over teaching science which is determined by self-efficacy – a person's beliefs about his or her own ability to perform a certain action – and perceived dependence on context factors; for example, the time allocated to teaching science in schools as discussed earlier on in this chapter, might very well be a contributing factor, alongside statutory requirements of the national curriculum for science and teachers' science subject knowledge (Wellcome 2015).

Therefore, as a student teacher of primary science, ask yourself how you can pro-actively combat these attitudes if you hold them? The first step is admitting or recognizing that you might hold one or more of the above. What support does your university or school provide for you to overcome these attitudes if you hold them?

What are primary schools *doing well* when teaching science and what can schools do to combat the issues highlighted?

As a trainee primary science teacher and hopefully future science leader, it's important to be aware of what schools do well, to incorporate into your own pedagogical practice, and know what challenges remain so you can do what you can, as a future classroom teacher and leader, to eradicate them.

In 2011, Ofsted released a report which evaluated the strengths and weaknesses of science education in England between 2007 and 2010, in both primary and secondary schools. In addition, in 2013, Ofsted's report – Maintaining Curiosity, examined science education in schools. More recently, the Welcome Trust Primary Science Campaign published the 'State of the nation' report of UK primary science education (CFE, 2017), important outcomes for you to consider from these reports are as follows:

Subject knowledge and teaching confidence

- In the primary schools visited; teachers' subject knowledge was at least satisfactory, in around 75 per cent of schools graded good to outstanding; however, teachers had concerns about their knowledge of physics and living things – limited expertise and confidence in teaching these areas of science restricted the level of challenge that some teachers could provide for the more academically able pupils (Wellcome 2014; CBI 2015).

- The reports noted that there was a lack of confidence of some primary teachers in teaching science which hindered the progress of the pupils they taught (Sharp, Hopkin and Lewthwait, 2011). The CFE (2017) found that 25 per cent of teachers were concerned that they might not be able to answer children's questions in science lessons with 21 per cent of teachers reporting that they neither agreed nor disagreed that they felt confident teaching science. Therefore, Senior Management Teams (SLT) should make provision for effective continuing professional development to support teachers' knowledge, understanding and skills in science so that they teach the correct conceptual science and do not create scientific misconceptions (Allen 2014) while improving teachers' confidence in teaching science.

Provision of science – planning and teaching

- In 80 per cent of the primary schools visited, the curriculum in science was good or outstanding; activities planned supported pupils' progress in their knowledge and understanding of science while allowing children to develop their science skills.

- The curriculum was often planned collaboratively with the children's interests in mind and planned to have a cross-curricular impact to develop other areas of the curriculum. Planned activities generally related well to objectives and practical activities stimulated pupil's engagement and enjoyment. However, in a minority of schools, there were weaknesses in

Figure 2.3 A year 3 child is developing his conceptual understanding of the phases of the moon

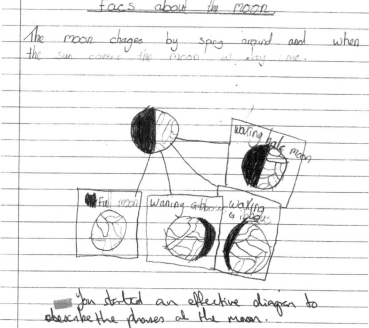

Figure 2.4 This activity focused on collaborative learning which the children were clearly engaged in and enjoyed

LO. To be able to understand the difference between series and parallel circuits.

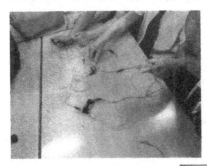 

The circuit below is a
Series circuit

In this lesson we Worked together to create a Series circuit. We made 3 light bulbs work and we had no arguing. We also created a parallel circuit, as we worked together we had fun

The circuit on the right is a
parallel circuit.
Because it is not connected and is incomplet.

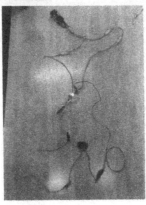 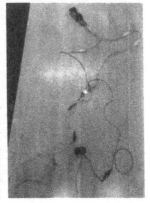

Figure 2.5 The written account of the investigation undertaken clearly has cross-curricular benefits; in this case writing

To be able to demonstrate knowledge of changing circuits.

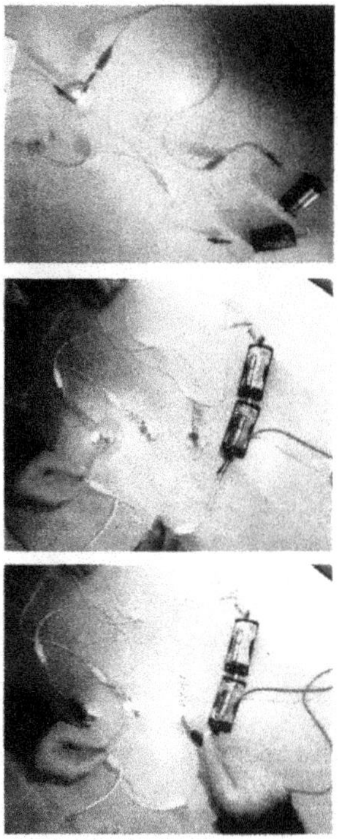

At the beginning we allocated different roles such as: the designer, builed technician, time keeper, scribes and resource manager. Our challenge was to make the 'wire up my car' challenge. We were brave enogh to attempt this challenge. What we needed to make use during this project was: light bolbs, wires, and paper clips for the switches. We tried don doing it diffrent ways, Each time we failed we did not moan, we tried it again and again. The designer desined diffrent ways to attempt the projects but when are group got it, time was up. We needed to change light bolbs because some of them did not work.

Your group worked very well together on understanding circuits.

Figure 2.6 Year 2 children grow cress seeds using varying materials before planting seeds in the school's allotment (as part of Gardening Club)

Figure 2.7 A thematic approach to the topic of water

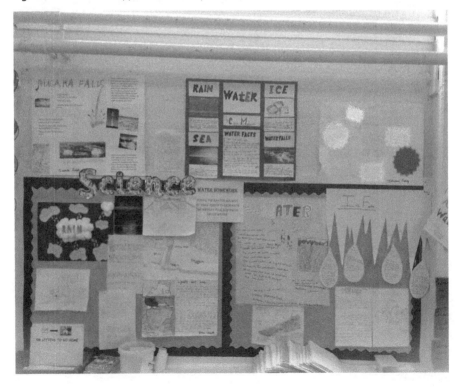

matching activities to pupils' prior learning so time was wasted or work was not completed and work restricted to a series of formulaic instructions inhibited independence.

- Strong links made between literacy and science contributed to achievement rising over time.

- Extra-curricular activities had a positive impact on pupils' attitudes to science and there was strong correlation between this and good to outstanding achievement. However, these activities were predominantly placed in biology.

- The most successful schools had moved away from schemes of work to adapting their own schemes of work to match pupils' needs and reflect the local environment – the curriculum was increasingly thematic which meant that science was taught less as a discrete subject; time was used more effectively where planning ensured the coverage of the national curriculum.

- Weaknesses were evident in some topic-based approaches that did not cover all the scientific content and process skills of the science programmes of study, for example IPC (Ofsted 2013).

Assessment

- Assessment was generally good or outstanding in around two thirds of schools visited; the guidance produced by the Qualifications and Curriculum Development Agency (QCDA) had not yet had a strong enough impact on schools' practice.

- The removal of the KS2 national tests had allowed some schools to provide year 6 pupils with a range of challenging science rather than being restricted to revising the science curriculum.

- Peer and Self-Assessment was evident in only a third of schools; in the best schools, target setting and next-step marking were identified as strategies which supported pupils in improving their work.

This has, no doubt, been compounded by the change in assessment procedures in primary schools. In May, 2013, the then secretary of state announced that as part of the reforms to the national curriculum, the 'levels' system used to report children's attainment in English, maths and science would be abolished and not replaced. This decision was informed by recommendations by the National Curriculum Expert Panel (2011) that schools should have the freedom to decide how to teach and assess the national curriculum.

We shall return to assessment and testing in Chapter 7, where we will explore how teachers can make use of a variety of effective assessment procedures to secure children's understanding in science.

Summary

The following table summarizes the current strengths and challenges for you to be aware of for your own practice and we have included outcomes, in relation to leadership, for readers of this book who aspire to be (or might already be) science leaders in primary schools.

Table 2.1 The provision of primary science in schools; strengths and challenges (Ofsted 2011: 2013; Wellcome Trust 2015: 2016; CFE, 2017)

Strengths – what schools do well	Challenges – what needs to be improved
• Planned activities relate well to learning objectives	• Time allocated to teaching science does not always reflect its core subject status
• Practical activities stimulate pupils' enjoyment and engagement	• Subject knowledge needs must be addressed in order for children to be more effectively challenged, especially the more academically able pupils
• Inclusion – barriers to learning are addressed	• Confidence in teaching pedagogy for some teachers needs to be addressed
• Social constructivism – to include all in learning science	
• The strong collaborative culture of primary schools – lessons are planned with the children's interests in mind and are planned to have a cross-curricular impact	• ICT needs to be used to challenge children and used to measure or record scientific enquiry by pupils
	• The assessment of scientific enquiry and process skills needs to be better developed
	• Programmes of study must be balanced providing children to develop both their conceptual understanding and scientific process skills
• Extra-curricular activities have a positive impact on pupils' attitudes to science as do school trips and outdoor learning	• Some children can find conceptual science difficult to understand; careful planning is required to address this
• Schools have created their own schemes of work to reflect their children's needs – personalized learning is valued	• CPD – science coordinators need training to enable them to become science specialists
• Science planned in curriculums that are thematic enable cross-curricular links to be made	• Links between primary and secondary schools need to be stronger; this would address access for primary teachers to specialist science teachers and enable a smoother transition between primary and secondary schools; secondary school teachers need to be clear on assessment procedures in primary schools
• Strong links between literacy and science contributed to achievement rising over time	
• The removal of KS2 tests enables teachers to provide year 6 pupils with a range of challenging science rather than being restricted to revision	• Assessment Beyond Levels has been problematic for some primary schools, leading to inconsistencies in assessment
	• Resources – schools need to invest more in resources for teaching science
• Science coordinators have been employed to lead primary science	• Schools need to value science education – monitoring of pupil progress and setting targets in science is not seen as a priority for some schools

- The teaching and learning of primary science has much improved since the introduction of the National Curriculum almost thirty years ago but still has improvements to make regarding the provision of primary science;
- Children's attitudes to active enquiry are positive although they can struggle with understanding some aspects of conceptual science, especially those which are counter-intuitive;
- As a teacher, how you feel about science will directly impact on your teaching of it!

Recommended reading

Allen, M. (2016). *The Best Ways to Teach Primary Science: Research into Practice.* Open University Press.

Harlen W. and Qualter, A. (2014). *The Teaching of Science in Primary Schools.* David Fulton.

Loxley, P. and Dawes, L. (2013). *Teaching Primary Science: Promoting Enjoyment and Developing Understanding.* Routledge.

Ofsted. (2011). *Successful Science; Strengths and Weaknesses of School Science Teaching.* Available at https://www.gov.uk/government/publications/successful-science-strengthes-and-weaknesses-of-school-science-teaching

Ofsted. (2013). *Not Yet Good Enough; Personal; Social, Health and Economic Education in Schools.* Manchester, Ofsted.

Ofsted. (2015). School Inspection Handbook. Available at https://www.gov.uk/government/ publications/ school-inspection-handbook-from- september-2015

Peacock, G. and Sharp, J. (2017). *Primary Science: Knowledge and Understanding (Achieving QTS series).* Sage.

Ward, H. and Roden, J. (2016). *Teaching Science in the Primary Classroom.* Sage.

Chapter 3
Science as an Irresistible Activity

Science, my lad, is made up of mistakes, but they are mistakes which it is useful to make because they lead little by little to the truth.

Jules Verne, *A Journey to the Centre of the Earth*

Chapter Objectives

By the end of this chapter you will have an understanding of:

- What creativity means in science
- What this might look like in the classroom
- Ways in which you could be a creative science teacher

Introduction

In Chapter 3, we examine what it is that makes science so appealing to many children, and ways in which you, as reflective practitioners, can make it more so. We have taken the view throughout this book that effective teaching relies on the constructivist and social-constructivist approach, and that to foster growth mindsets in the children is an important part of developing positive attitudes to science. By taking ownership of your teaching, letting loose your creative side, you will be able to foster creativity in children's approach to problem-solving in a way that will bring extreme satisfaction to both you and the children.

Children have an irresistible urge to find out information and to understand the world they live in, and we can choose to either foster that innate desire, or we can squash it, and in effect, make learning a passive affair in which children have no agency.

This chapter explores ways in which we can create meaningful and irresistible learning experiences for the children, while at the same time ensuring that children are making progress with the 'soft skills' needed to approach the world in which they will take their place as informed citizens. We look at how teachers can help the children begin to join up the thinking and knowing about the world in ways that make science an exciting and interesting endeavour that resonates with the children's lived experiences. This not only engages the children with their learning, but also makes your job more pleasurable and satisfying.

What is creativity in primary science teaching?

Creativity is piercing the mundane to find the marvellous. (Bill Moyers)

When you think of science, what do you think of? Do you think about the science you did at school? Some of you may remember science as boring, difficult to understand and not relevant. Why do you think that was the case? Some of you, however, may remember your school science as exciting and fun and that you looked forward to science lessons. What was it about those lessons that made them exciting? If you fall into the 'science is boring; all facts and results' camp, let us try and convince you otherwise.

Pause for thought

Think of some famous scientists you may know. They could be from the past or present day. What were their discoveries? Can you remember the stories of how they got started on their discoveries?

The NACCCE Report (1999) defined creativity as having four main components: using the imagination, pursuing with purpose, being original and judging value. Think again about your famous scientist. Did he or she have creativity based on these factors? Maybe you thought about Sir Isaac Newton and the traditional tale of the apple falling from the tree sparking his imagination and his ideas about gravity, for example. Case study 3.1 gives you a more recent example of creativity in science.

CASE STUDY 3.1: The story of Graphene

Professor Andre Geim and Professor Kostya Novoselov of Manchester University frequently held 'Friday night experiments', when they would investigate science not necessarily to do with their day jobs. On one such Friday night, in 2003, they removed some flakes from a lump of bulk graphite (the same graphite that is in your pencils) with humble sticky tape. They noticed that some of the flakes were thinner than others, and by separating the graphite fragments repeatedly they managed to create flakes that were just one atom thick. They had isolated graphene for the first time. This playful approach is fundamental to how the two scientists work. It is seen as a useful way of maintaining interest, as well as a means of generating new ideas. The tradition of Friday night experiments continues with all the University of Manchester graphene researchers.

The amazing properties of graphene were identified through repeated experimentation on this 2D material. It is 200 times stronger than steel, yet incredibly flexible; it is the thinnest material possible and is transparent; it is the world's most conductive material yet it can act as a barrier – not even helium can pass through it. The two scientists were awarded a Nobel Prize in 2010 for their discovery.

How does this story resonate with the factors for creativity identified by NACCCE (1999)?

Of course, in the primary classroom, children and teachers are not necessarily dealing with game changing science like the case study above, so where does creativity come into primary science? According to NACCCE (1999), creativity can and should be developed in all areas of school life (and beyond), which includes science and it includes teaching. Oliver (2006) suggests that much of primary school science focuses on the teaching and learning of knowledge, identifying factors and looking for cause and effect, the so-called fair test. She goes on to say that there is a huge potential to build on what is happening in schools by following [children's] ideas, responding to their curiosity and questioning their beliefs. That, in our view, is being creative.

Pause for thought

Think about people you know who are creative, in, for example, art, music, cooking or a hobby:

- What makes them creative?
- Are the attributes for creativity that you have listed different for science?
- When do you demonstrate your creativity?

Davies (2011) talks of two aspects of creativity in primary science: teaching creatively and teaching *for* creativity, which could be viewed as the teaching and learning of science.

Craft (2004) recognizes that 'a pedagogy which fosters creativity depends on practitioners being creative to provide the ethos for enabling children's creativity' (Craft 2005: 44) suggesting that Davies' two aspects are mutually dependent.

Teaching *for* creativity will be addressed further in chapters 4 and 6. Davies goes on to identify some of the dimensions for creative practice that he adapted from Granger et al. (2006). Cremin et al. (2006) have suggested that creative practice is developed from three interdependent dimensions, which are summarized in Table 3.1 below.

You may think that you're not a creative person, but if you try to plan exciting lessons that 'hook' the children in, that are contextually relevant to their lives, and that engage and motivate them; if you like trying new things, and aren't afraid when things don't work out quite as you expected, then you probably are quite creative!

Creativity is about being open to the changing nature of science, and giving some of the control in the classroom back to the children, so that they feel secure in asking questions and deciding which questions they can investigate. It's about letting go and letting them plan the kind of investigation they think will answer those questions. This can be hard to do in an outcomes-driven environment, because as they learn to 'be scientists' children will inevitably make some mistakes along the way, but vital if we are to foster a growth mindset (Dweck 2012). We need to celebrate when the results of investigations don't match the predictions, as of course it raises more questions, and they've discovered something unexpected. We need to help children believe in themselves, and that they themselves can figure out what to do to make their investigations better. This idea of children questioning their results and seeking answers links well with the discussion on scientific literacy in Chapter 1.

Table 3.1 Dimensions of creative practice, from Davies (2011)

Personal Qualities	Pedagogy	Classroom and School Ethos
• Commitment to children	• Using diverse teaching methods	• Environment reflects positive values
• Desire to learn	• Identifying entry points for individuals	• Environment promotes emotional engagement
• Flexibility and enthusiasm	• Linking ideas	• Pupils feel safe, valued and trusted
• Risk-taking and curiosity	• Connecting with pupils' lives	• Pupils encouraged to speculate and take risks
• Undertaking children's needs and interests	• Using ICT	• Appropriate resources provided
• Using humour	• Adopting a questioning stance	• Links with the wider community
• Secure knowledge base	• Encouraging children to ask questions	• Supportive leadership
	• Encouraging independence	
	• Working together	

Besides, young children aren't afraid to fail. Watch any toddler learning to walk and falling on their bottoms – they soon get back up and try again until they've mastered the skill. Children in the Early Years and Foundation Stage will explore the water or sand tray over and over again, until they are satisfied with what they are investigating. Why do children lose that focus and persistence in school, and start being afraid to get things wrong? Is it the culture of prescribed outcomes that meet learning objectives that is stifling creativity? Sir Ken Robinson (https://www.ted.com/talks/ken_robinson_says_schools_kill_creativity) says so. He believes that schools, by their very nature, are killing creativity.

How does creativity help to make science irresistible?

Play is a large part of the received pedagogy in the Early Years and Foundation Stage classrooms. It is underpinned by Piaget's theory of children learning through the interaction with their environment. Indeed, Piaget saw young children as 'lone scientists' ploughing their way again and again through multitudes of experiences in order to make sense of the world. As children move through the primary years, play takes more and more of a back seat, until by year 6, learning is a serious business. We don't mean to imply that learning shouldn't be taken seriously, by practitioners or the learners; quite the reverse. Strong subject knowledge and a serious consideration of high expectations are vital. However, we believe that the playfulness that characterizes the work of Geim and Novoselov and their amazing discovery can be enthusiastically promoted in our primary classrooms, and it's done through creative planning and teaching and teaching for creativity, which as previously mentioned will be addressed in more detail in forthcoming chapters.

Many children, despite the apparent trend towards teaching the most basic knowledge and skills required by the curriculum, enjoy science in primary schools. Effective science teaching and learning has the power to engage children in exciting and creative learning.

The creative teacher will be able to make science irresistible to the children by giving them ownership and responsibility for their science. Of course, we don't mean let the children do whatever they like. The teacher still has responsibility to make sure that the curriculum is covered, and that process and enquiry skills are learnt and that progression in the skills and concepts is monitored; however, as Creative Scotland (2013) found, children are more likely to find science is irresistible if we give them the power. According to Creative Scotland, this is achieved by accepting the greatest resource is the learner and if you are able to pay attention and listen to them, then the curriculum is brought to life in their curiosity and persistence. Through this approach, children make their own connections to previous learning, and using imagination, are able to think creatively.

CASE STUDY 3.2: Creative Scotland (2013)

Creative Scotland (2013) in their report found that pupils responded positively to their enhanced agency to direct and shape their own learning. In all the classrooms we worked in, we observed a natural order emerging among the pupils after an initial, excited period of chatter. The pupils naturally gravitated from talking, listening and reflecting, towards wanting to action their ideas. Traditional ideas of classroom management often reinforce the dominance of the teacher who dictates the pace and direction of the learning, or the deeply ingrained assumption that they have to.

Our experiments demonstrated how, when afforded the time, space and responsibility, pupils can organize themselves and enthusiastically structure their own, personally meaningful learning. This sort of enhanced pupil agency frees the teacher to become a facilitator, able to encourage and help to focus the learning that is naturally taking place. We don't suggest that this should be the way every classroom should work, every day of the week, but certainly the pupils demonstrated their enthusiasm and capabilities for making more use of enhanced pupil agency.

What is your experience of pupil agency in the classroom?

To what extent does your practice fit the traditional idea of didactic teaching?

The intrinsic reward to both children and the teacher, of this sometimes fearful pedagogy of letting go of some of the control in the classroom, is the fostering of the 'growth mindset' (Dweck) already mentioned, where children are not afraid of making mistakes, but see them as an essential part of learning. This idea also sits well with Piaget's notion of schema and of cognitive conflict and that of transformative learning through the process of accommodation and assimilation leading to equilibrium. Transformative learning could be described as deep learning where ideas have been changed or added to as a result of the cognitive conflict.

Ask anyone who has spent time with young children, and they will concur with the fact that they are always asking 'why?'. Finding out the answers is in itself irresistible to children, although as has been discussed already, the spontaneous asking of questions and creativity in finding the answers seems to wane considerably as children make their way through primary school. But children in year 6 are still naturally drawn to intriguing situations, in our experience, and the creative practitioner, who can plan intriguing lessons that draw the children in, is making science irresistible to children. This might at first seem a daunting task, but it is not so difficult if you adopt the characteristics summarized in Table 3.1 (Holligan 2013). The hands-on practical approach to science is a great leveller during which all children can engage and learn in their own way, and, to our minds takes no longer to prepare than the worksheet differentiated three ways – surely the ultimate nail in the coffin of creativity.

Johnson (2005: 88) argues that *'creative science educational experiences have three essential elements: they should be practical, memorable and interactive'*.

Furthermore, she recommends that subject knowledge and pedagogical knowledge should be adapted to suit the needs of individual children, the context and the learning objectives (Johnson 2005 cited in Davies 2011).

Why should science be an irresistible activity?

Science is important because we need to nurture the next generations of scientists (Roden and Archer 2014). Although as has been discussed, children enjoy science (Archer et al. 2103), there seems to be a reluctance among young people to go into occupations that use the sciences. If we are to aspire people to go into science, then we need to make it an enjoyable and irresistible subject for them.

Not only that, as creative teachers, we need to help children see the value of science and how it relates to their everyday lives. Indeed, we need to make the links for them so that they understand that science underpins our everyday lives, as has been discussed in Chapter 1. So, our job is to plan and deliver imaginative and inspiring learning opportunities.

In our PGCE science sessions, the students always get the opportunity to 'play' with trays of science equipment before getting down to the important business of planning lessons and revising subject knowledge. Evaluations of the sessions consistently evidence how enjoyable these sessions are to them. *'I always get so interested in everything; I've always been free to play'* (Miriam Rothschild 1997, quoted in Oliver 2006) If that is the case for adults, how much more engaging and enjoyable must it be for children to get to do practical, hands-on activities in their science lessons? The teacher, however, as a guide to the children's explorations and learning, must ensure that the children are not only hands-on, but also minds-on to the science underpinning these learning opportunities.

Children learn through their experiences, and according to Piaget, as has been mentioned, if those experiences create some cognitive conflict that needs to be assimilated and accommodated to create cognitive equilibrium, then deep learning can occur. That old chestnut attributed to Confucius of 'I hear and I forget, I do and I remember', has resonance with primary science. The important point here about the constructivist approach to learning is that by assimilating new information into existing schema, or by creating new schemas, then conceptual change occurs, and thus cognitive development: learning. It is the intriguing situations, the puzzle when things don't turn out in the expected way, and the search for answers that make science so irresistible to children.

A caveat here, though, is that children sometimes, despite the evidence, have a wonderful capacity to continue to hold their original (sometimes called naïve or incomplete) ideas firmly, and sometimes even alongside more 'scientific' explanations. Indeed, many adults also do this. How many of you reading this have mothers who have told them not to go out with wet hair or they will catch a cold? Most of you, we imagine. Of course, the scientific explanation is that a virus causes a cold, and it has nothing to do with being wet or cold, but we continue to believe it, and indeed, pass it on down the generations! (Shulman and Valcarcel 2012).

Of course, it is evident that to create these wonderful conditions for learning, children have to practise not getting the answers 'right', and that it is acceptable for their investigations to give unexpected results. To do that, the teacher must create a safe and secure learning environment, where 'mistakes' are viewed as fantastic learning opportunities, because the children get to do more investigating. Enjoyment breeds more engagement and motivation, which in turn breeds more enjoyment. What's not to like? That's one more reason why science in the primary classroom needs to be irresistible.

What does science look like as an irresistible activity?

What does a classroom where science is an irresistible activity look like? What will be happening and who is in charge? Hopefully, science activities start with some excited chatter as children and teachers wonder why …? With luck, you'll see a wonder wall display that is filled with post-it notes of the children's questions, which demonstrates children's natural curiosity and willingness to find explanations for the world around them.

If you're in an early years classroom (and maybe in year 1) you'll see a role play area that is a rich source of science exploration: a mechanic's workshop with opportunities to explore forces, a space rocket that has the components of a circuit for the astronauts to make the bulbs and buzzers work. Children will still be chattering excitedly about what they have found out.

In primary classrooms, children will be working collaboratively in mixed-ability groupings, which draw on the social-constructivist principles of shared understandings and peer scaffolding with More Knowledgeable Others scaffolding the learning of those with less knowledge. Children will be engaged in cumulative talk (Howe and Mercer 2007), which moves all their science understanding on.

Where children are engaged in irresistible science, they will be involved in exploration, problem-solving, designing experiments and drawing conclusions which they share with their peers (Cutting and Kelly 2015). In other words, children are asking questions and purposefully planning how they will find out the answers, confidently using a range of investigations and equipment. Children are excited when they get unexpected results, because they have more questions, more thinking to do and more investigating. Because the science is relevant to their lives, and they have ownership of their learning, they are learning to look at the mundane in a different way – through the eyes of scientists – and it is exciting to them.

The 2013 Curriculum for Primary Science states that the purpose of science study is to *'develop a sense of excitement and curiosity about natural phenomena'* (Science programme of study: key stages 1 and 2, 2013). It also goes on to state that insecure, superficial understanding will not allow genuine progression in conceptual understanding. In a didactic classroom, where knowledge is imparted by the teacher, or the teacher plans the investigations giving little ownership to the children, deep learning is unlikely to occur. Furthermore, the preamble to the curriculum states clearly that most of the science should be done through the use of first-hand practical experiences. We would argue that where schools are intent of developing children's writing, and science is used as a thinly veiled opportunity to do yet more writing, then those schools are not fulfilling the statutory requirements (see Chapter 2 for further discussion about this distressing occurrence in some schools). As it is, the 2013 curriculum could be seen as a wonderful opportunity for truly creative learning to take place, as long as the science is still rigorous, and the timetable allows the space.

CASE STUDY 3.3

In year 5, an ex-student of ours has invested a lot of time into making her science lessons both creative and relevant to the children. Using the most topical subject of the refugee crisis, children were asked what they thought the refugees needed most. Among other ideas, the children responded that clean water and suitable shelter were urgent needs. The teacher helped the children to turn these into questions that could be investigated in science, and they developed both enquiry skills and concept knowledge by planning and carrying out investigations about cleaning water and choosing appropriate materials to manufacture tents.

What makes this teaching and learning particularly creative, we believe, is that the teacher was not restricted to a 'topic' for the science, as in following the curriculum in a linear form, but allowing the children to choose what aspects of the chemistry strand to investigate themselves. Through careful monitoring across the year, the full curriculum can be addressed, but in a way that is immediate and relevant to what is going on in real life, and thus being able to address socioscientific aspects at the same time.

How can teachers make primary science irresistible?

To our minds, the most important thing that teachers can do to make science irresistible to children is to find it irresistible themselves. What we mean is that teachers have to have passion and enthusiasm and to share this openly with the children. It seems logical to us that if their teacher is full of wonder at the marvellous things science has to offer, and is excited, then so will the children be.

Oliver (2006) gives a useful check-list of things that creative science teachers do to make science irresistible.

- Provide challenging activities
- Give children time to talk
- Share and generate ideas
- Encourage independent exploration and discovery
- Value speculation and original thinking
- Help pupils make useful connections
- Give permission to try something new, take risks
- Encourage wonder, curiosity and spontaneity
- Follow children's ideas purposefully
- Accept individual routes to learning
- Show flexibility in their thinking
- Opt for alternative non-routine approaches
- Encourage complexity as a way of stimulating interest

Pause for thought

- Think about the science lessons you have taught. Which of the above list could you apply to your lessons?
- How could you make your science teaching more creative?
- Have you been able to use the children's ideas to plan subsequent learning, for example?

If you look back to the quote at the beginning of this chapter, Bill Moyers, says that to be creative, we need to make things marvellous and lift them from the mundane. One way to interpret that is for us as teachers to encourage children to look again at everyday experiences and knowledge and to see the marvel of science. For example, using visualizers and digital microscopes (and nearly all schools have these nowadays) to show children what things look like when magnified. Simple magnifying glasses that allow the children to really observe closely, and to experience the wonder of, say the underside of a leaf or a butterfly's wings make observing truly marvellous!

Most of the children we teach now are very comfortable using tablets and if your school has tablets for the children to use, there are a plethora of science apps that can be downloaded to use in the classroom. Some can involve the children in being 'real-life' scientists taking part in large studies such as the RSPB's Birdwatch. This adds to the excitement of what could be quite a mundane experience such as recognizing and classifying British birds, which additionally may not be relevant to many urban children. It's that bit more relevant if your observations are part of a 'citizen science' data gathering exercise!

As discussed previously, giving the children more ownership of their science, from planning their own investigations, choosing appropriate equipment and trying it out, and going outside of the classroom for part of their science all make the whole learning experience much more exciting – so different from many of the other subject lessons that children have to endure, with their emphasis on the evidence in books. Creative teaching is about making the children's learning a rich and meaningful experience, and the rewards are manifold.

Creative teachers will find intriguing hooks to draw children towards the learning, and to make it more meaningful. For example, using stories to foster interest can create a meaningful and playful way into a topic. Stories can encourage children to ask questions about the story topic and are also useful for providing a context of why they should investigate and explore particular phenomena. Models and analogies (despite their limitations) can help children to make connections between abstract, unobservable concepts with something demonstrable. According to Cross and Board (2014), making creative comparisons between things we don't understand and things that we do understand is a powerful way of making sense of the world around us.

A vital tool for creative teaching is, of course, strong subject knowledge. If you're going to be open to deep rather than surface learning, that is not dependent on written evidence, or all children meeting the predictable learning objectives lesson by lesson, you will need to understand the 'big' ideas of science (Harlen 2010), and the foundations that we lay down in the early years and primary education.

CASE STUDY 3.4: Year 1 Invertebrates

In a school that insisted on written evidence of all learning, Claire was on her final PGCE school experience in the summer term. Looking through the children's science books, she was horrified to notice that in the whole academic year so far, they had only conducted one investigation. The school had recently laid tarmac down in what had been a lovely wildlife area because the children would bring mud into the school after break-time. How was she to teach engaging and exciting lessons with a focus on investigation? She decided on a 'mini-beast hunt' in the erstwhile wildlife area, to look at habitats, but evidently this was going to be difficult with not many differing conditions. However, being creative, she cut out and laminated pictures of a variety of invertebrates, and hid them around the area, on trees, under stones, in dark and damp places, etc.

During her whole class input, Claire asked the children to predict where they thought the invertebrates might be found. The children did not know the word predict, so some time was spent explaining what she meant, and then many children were able to use their prior knowledge to discuss where they thought the most invertebrates would be found.

The enthusiasm and excitement was palpable when she explained that they were to be scientists and investigate where the invertebrates lived, which was not only to find the creatures hidden in various places, but to place them in hoops on the floor labelled with the various areas, to easily ascertain the most favoured habitats. Some children were able to name some of the invertebrates she had hidden.

> The class teacher was so impressed with the quality of the written work the children produced, that she photocopied some to send home to parents! One child in his work about habitats had written that some bees lived in hives and made honey, so the very next week, Claire chose a non-fiction book about bees, for literacy, and among other activities, the children researched how vital the bees are for our crops.
>
> From an unpromising start, Claire had planned and delivered an exciting, engaging and marvellous lesson.
>
> What made it creative? Look back to Table 3.1 to remind yourself of some of the attributes of creative practitioners.

Above all, remember: make it marvellous!

A society's competitive advantage will come not from how well its schools teach the multiplication and periodic tables, but from how well they stimulate imagination and creativity. (Albert Einstein)

Summary

- What creativity is and how it helps to make science irresistible.
- Why science should be an irresistible activity.
- What science looks like when it's irresistible.
- How you as a teacher can make science irresistible to both children and yourself.

Recommended reading

Inspiring Einstein Minds. Beggs, J., Murphy, C. and Kerr, K. (2009). Primary Science No 109. Available at www.ase.org.uk

Cutting, R. and Kelly, O. (2015). *Creative Teaching in Primary Science.* London: Sage.

Creativity for a Purpose. Ward, H. (2011). Primary Science No 119 Available at www.ase.org.uk

The Art of Chemistry. Rivett, A. C., Harrison, T. G. and Shallcross, D. E. (2009). Primary Science No 110. Available at www.ase.org.uk

http://www.graphene.manchester.ac.uk/explore/the-story-of-graphene/global-explosion/

http://www.ted.com/talks/ken_robinson_says_schools_kill_creativity

http://www.rspb.org.uk

www.creative-little-scientists.eu

Ofsted. (2013). Maintaining Curiosity: A survey into science education in schools. Available at www.gov.uk

Chapter 4
Science as a Practical Activity

The scientist is not a person who gives the right answers, he's the one who asks the right questions.

Claude Lévi-Strauss

Chapter objectives

By the end of this chapter, you will have explored and thus gained an understanding of:

- What is meant by 'working scientifically'.
- Why learning through enquiry is important.
- Why the process skills are important.
- What are the roles that practical work plays in progress of skills.
- How talk develops science understanding.
- How using enquiry skills can develop children's autonomy.

Introduction

This chapter will give you insight into why it is so important for children to be actively involved with learning science by *doing* science and finding out the answers to their own questions about the world. Of course, in the setting of the primary school, it doesn't mean that children can come up with any old question, and that they can then go about finding the answers in a random way. It is about developing more and more scientific ways of asking questions that can be tested, and it is about learning that to be valid, the data has to be valid and that the evidence can be respected. This chapter links with ideas in other chapters that discuss the importance of children developing their scientific literacy in order to become informed citizens, and explores the ways that this can happen.

The importance of science as a practical endeavour rather than the passive receipt of knowledge passed from teacher to child is discussed, and the importance of children talking and collaborating with one another in the classroom is explored as a vital tool for the development of children's cognitive development and as a means to encourage transformative learning, alongside the development of the key skills that children will need in order to move towards a more scientific way of engaging with problems. Chapter 4 is about encouraging children to take an active role in thinking about the world they live in, it's about asking relevant questions about the science that can explain everyday phenomena that children experience, and it's about how to find out the answers to those questions in a systematic and meaningful way.

What is enquiry learning in science?

Science enquiry is what children do in order to answer scientific questions about the world around them. (Turner et al. 2011: 11)

The difference between a general enquiry (asking a question such as where is my pencil?) and a scientific enquiry is very much to do with the way in which the question is answered. If science is about the world around them, and children are engaged in trying to find out answers to questions about the world, then the finding out can be considered 'scientific enquiry'.

There is some debate about the use of the word 'enquiry' or 'inquiry'. The generally accepted dictionary explanation of the difference between the two is that an enquiry is a more general question and inquiry is a more formalized way of going about answering the question through investigation. However, in practice, it seems right to refer to scientific *enquiry* in primary settings as certainly to begin with children are asking more general questions and aren't yet skilled enough to answer the questions systematically and the answers their enquiry presents them with is not yet evidence in the way that a more formal research scientist might view it. Children at primary level need to find a suitable outcome to their questions, for example finding an explanation that satisfies them in terms of their cognitive developmental level or that raises yet more questions.

Therefore, in the primary context, what is scientific enquiry? Well, it is children being involved in different types of investigations, contextualized in the topics of the National Curriculum and more, while at the same time developing all the skills associated with working 'like scientists' (Cross and Bowden 2014). The national curriculum for England (DfE 2013) includes the overarching strand of 'working scientifically', which by its name suggests the expectation that children will develop these skills over their primary career and become increasingly scientific in their endeavours. Perhaps, we could say they increasingly work towards 'inquiries' rather than 'enquiries'. What is clear is that it is the teachers' responsibility to plan for a wide variety of experiences that will develop these scientific skills, at the same time as developing their conceptual knowledge and understanding of how the world works.

What exactly do we mean by scientific enquiry?

Scientific enquiry is a practical activity through which knowledge and understanding of scientific concepts (e.g. light, the digestive system, gravity, states of matter) are learnt. What is important here is that it is the 'doing' of science enquiry that goes hand in hand with the development of the conceptual knowledge and understanding about the 'big ideas' in science (Harlen 2010), that is, neither can be learnt in isolation of the other.

The important aspects involved with scientific enquiry include:

- Making observations
- Asking questions
- Researching from secondary sources
- Planning a variety of investigations
- Reviewing what is already known
- Using different methods to gather, analyse and interpret data
- Putting forward tentative answers and explanations that suggest predictions and
- Communicating the results in different ways

As children have experience of all of the above aspects of enquiry over time, higher-order thinking (Bloom's revised taxonomy, 2001) develops and requires children to begin to identify assumptions, use critical and logical thinking, and to consider alternative explanations for outcomes. The skills that children need to develop in order to undertake scientific enquiry will be considered in section 4.

Pause for thought

- What scientific enquiry is not:

    One or two pupils were involved in demonstrating their understanding of a nutritionally balanced meal by assembling a meal on a plate from a selection of different food types while the rest [of the pupils] just sat on the carpet and watched and drifted away. Others had to record the results of a teacher demonstration that took 25 minutes, recording (but not measuring for themselves) a temperature every minute!

    (Ofsted 2013:12)

- Does this resonate with any science lessons you have observed?
- Have you planned any lessons like this?

Different kinds of science questions and contexts mean that in order to find answers and explanations, different types of enquiry are needed. There are five main forms of science enquiry that are listed in the National Curriculum (2013), and which require teachers to ensure a balance over the course of each academic year.

They are:

- Fair Testing
- Classifying and Identifying
- Pattern Seeking
- Observing over time
- Research

However, many teachers, it seems, resort to a limited default position of planning for children to engage in fair testing (Dunne and Makland 2015), which may be attributed to teachers finding science 'hard' (Peacock and Dunne 2015). That is to say, teachers whose confidence in their subject knowledge and understanding of 'doing science' may well fall back on 'recipe science' (Abrahams and Reiss 2012), in which children are over guided into doing what the teacher intends, with the expected outcomes. This is quite likely as a result of an accountability culture in schools, where all children need to give evidence of meeting the learning objective in every lesson, whether they have actually learnt anything or not!

Indeed, in our own visits to schools when supervising students we have more than once come across experienced teachers who try to 'shoehorn' a fair test where it is not appropriate to the situation. On one memorable occasion, a teacher tried to convince the supervisor that looking at the length of dandelion leaves on the school field was a fair test type of investigation.

Pause for thought

Spend some time thinking about the investigations you have planned for the children in your class. Have you helped the children to ask questions that can be investigated using the full range of science enquiry methods? Which ones do you feel most confident about?

Why is learning through enquiry important?

One of the most widely known views of learning is that of constructivism as mooted by Jean Piaget (1973). Piaget's view of how learning occurs is that children are active builders of knowledge; they are little scientists who construct their own theories of the world.

That is, they investigate the world through interaction with their experiences, hypothesizing and testing out situations. Piaget believed that we all search for cognitive equilibrium, and that when challenged with information that could not be readily assimilated into pre-existing schemata, cognitive conflict or 'disequilibrium' would occur, causing the mind to accommodate the information through the formation of new schemata to restore equilibrium. The SPACE Reports (1990–1998) found that learning occurs when children engage in new experiences. They try to make sense of what is happening by drawing on knowledge that they already have, making predictions based on their ideas, and test them to see if they fit the predictions. If it does, then the idea becomes a little 'bigger', but if it doesn't work, then a new idea has to be tried. This idea sits very well with the constructivist approach mooted by Piaget, don't you think?

The notion of testing not working out in the way it was predicted is an interesting one. 'Ah!' I hear you say, 'but children don't like to get things wrong and it can damage their self-esteem, put them off trying, and they don't engage. Let's make sure we are scaffolding their success'. Well the thing about science is that the knowledge that is generally accepted as 'scientific fact' is only as much as the science community has agreed is the extent of our understanding at this moment in time. If further evidence came to light, then we might just agree that we were 'wrong' and change our understandings to fit the new evidence. An example of this scientific thinking using new evidence might be found if we contemplate Einstein's Theory of Relativity and the work now being done at CERN with the Large Hadron Collider there which is shedding some doubt that Einstein's theory goes far enough.

Thus, one of the important things about scientific enquiry in the primary school is that we as practitioners must encourage children to believe that if their investigation didn't uphold their predictions, then that's fantastic, because we have the opportunity to learn something new. If predictions are upheld, then it just confirms to the children what they already knew. The fostering of positive attitudes and growth mindsets (Dweck 2012) is a vital component of scientific enquiry. How many of you have already encountered children trying to 'rub out' their predictions if they don't match the evidence of the investigation?

Besides, the wonderful thing about predictions that don't work out is that they encourage yet more questions, and without a question to find answers to or explanations for, there would be no scientific enquiry.

CASE STUDY 4.1: How do we encourage children to ask scientific questions?

In year 2, the teacher read the children 'Yucky Worms' by Vivian French, a story about worms with facts alongside. In the outdoor space, children were looking for worms as they had become so interested and began asking questions such as, 'where do worms live', 'how do they move?' and others. The children spent time finding worms in the garden and observing how they moved using magnifying glasses. This raised more questions about the anatomy of worms ('what is the saddle' for?' for example. The teacher responded to their questions and planned a research investigation into the anatomy of a worm, and brought in a 'wormery' so that the children could observe their behaviour and diet more readily. All the children were fascinated to watch the worms making worm casts and tunnels through the soil. This work then gave opportunities for literacy work when the children wrote the diary of a worm and their own worm stories.

The important thing about the above case study is that it was situated within a topic about variation, it 'hooked' the children in and got them thinking and asking questions, and it gave them opportunities for enquiry skills beyond the 'fair test'.

The important thing here is that children have questions to answer, and that it is they themselves who have thought of the question; that there is something that they want to know about. Anyone of us who have had dealings with young children knows that they are often asking 'why?' or 'how?' Children in upper primary ask less questions than in EYFS; why? Wurman (2000), the founder of Ted© Talks has focused on the educational system. 'In school, we're rewarded for having the answer, not for asking a good question.' What does school do to them? Could it be that in school we are predisposed to reward correct answers rather than the questions, and that it is the teachers asking the questions for assessment to check that the children understand our teaching? Could it also be that in many classrooms, teachers don't encourage children to ask questions in case they either can't answer them, or haven't got time to answer them in the 'hurry along curriculum'?

Furthermore, teachers are often under pressure to have planning for their lessons ready in advance, sometimes for the whole topic, but also weekly. There are obvious organizational benefits for this as teachers can ensure that the appropriate resources are prepared and available, and advance planning also ensures even coverage of science enquiry over the span of the year, but it certainly shuts down children's questions, ownership and engagement with the learning. Confidence in subject knowledge and the common ideas that children will bring to a topic can allow teachers to start a science topic with some exploration or observation to encourage children's questions which can be added to a 'working wall'.

So how can we encourage children to ask questions and to ensure that their questions become more scientific as they develop? Well the first thing we have to do, as in all our teaching, is to model our enthusiasm and to ask questions ourselves, especially the enquiry ones. But we also have to be brave and take on the idea that children will come up with some surprising theories. We have to be able to suspend judgement; that is to say, we need to value the ideas children have, and show them how to turn their ideas into questions that can be tested through scientific enquiry.

CASE STUDY 4.2

Years ago, as an NQT, Kenna was leading a class discussion on what the year 6 children thought was important for healthy plant growth. She was completely taken aback, when one girl said that she thought that trees needed concrete to grow in. At that time, she didn't have the experience to do more than valiantly add it to the list of factors. However, on reflecting later about what she should do about this surprising idea, she realized that in the social housing where this girl lived, a programme of 'greening up' the communal space had been embarked upon, and indeed when Kenna checked, squares of the concrete forecourt had been removed and trees had been planted in them. This reflective girl had been thinking about her own experience, and had hypothesized that if the parks department had planted trees in the concrete, then that was evidently what they needed! At the time, Kenna managed to get hold of some cement powder, and they duly planted a pot plant in it, to see what would happen.

As teachers, we need to give children time to explore and observe so that they start asking the questions, and, as they get more experienced in working scientifically, begin to make decisions about which kind of enquiry they should undertake in order to find out the answers to their own questions. Those of you who are lucky enough to be involved with the Forest Schools programme (Forest Schools Association), for example, will have plenty of opportunity to take your children outside, and to model the asking of questions about the natural world, from what you observe. Working alongside children in this way, so that you are learning together is a powerful pedagogical tool.

> A strong feature of the Early Years Foundation Stage was that teachers allowed children to complete the activity they had chosen; the older the pupils were, the less likely it was that they had the freedom to take time to explore ideas, find solutions and get to the bottom of their enquiry. (Ofsted 2013:19)

What skills do children need to develop in order to engage in scientific enquiry?

However, a word of caution here: even though children may be engaged in practical activities that are rooted in finding answers about the world, the enquiry may not justify the label of 'scientific enquiry'. This is because, despite being active, the children are not developing ideas from evidence, but are being told the answers to what happens and why. Understandably in our rather 'hurry along' curriculum, where teachers are anxious to demonstrate that they have covered the required curriculum for that particular term or year, many teachers plan the enquiry for the children, and indeed, tell children which variables to change and which to keep the same. This is often in the guise of 'scaffolding the learning' so that there are successful outcomes, whereby the teacher believes that the conceptual knowledge has been arrived at. In other words, there may be lots of action – observing and recording, even predicting, but not much use of the skills that engage their minds and develop their understanding. What is often missing then is the scientific thinking that uses evidence to test ideas.

> Thus [practical] work is not an add-on or distraction from content mastery, but rather one of many pathways to both factual knowledge and deeper conceptual understanding. (NRC 2005:10)

Children need to develop their scientific thinking. They need their teachers to effectively 'join up' their thinking so that they are clear about what they have learnt from their enquiries. Importantly, they need to be able to finish off their enquiries by thinking about what their evidence tells them, to evaluate their methodology, and to draw conclusions.

> The best schools made sure that pupils finished the work set, especially if it was a practical investigation. This led to some pupils continuing with the activity in the next lesson with different starting points for different pupils depending on the progress they had made previously. The more common alternative in science, however, was for all pupils to start something new in the next lesson. That undermined the importance of the original task and cemented a gap in pupils' learning. (Ofsted 2013:42)

What does progress in scientific enquiry and using the process skills look like?

If children are to develop their enquiry and process skills during the EYFS and primary years, then it is logical that they will need to practice them. No teacher would expect a child to be able to write in a beautiful fully cursive script without lots of practice, and it stands to reason that working scientifically, like any other skill, needs to be revisited again and again.

The tables below demonstrate how children's enquiry skills can be built on year on year, and move from early explorations and asking questions, to becoming increasingly more scientific and working as a scientist might (Cross and Bowden 2014). It is a simple way for teachers and subject leads to monitor the progress of children and to ensure that they have a full range of opportunities to engage in working scientifically. This strand of the National Curriculum (2013) is generally held to be an overarching strand which develops in tandem with the concepts. As a matter of fact, the preamble to the National Curriculum makes it very clear that enquiry cannot be taught, or learnt, without the context of the conceptual knowledge contained in the physics, biology and chemistry strands.

Table 4.1 Working Scientifically: Progression of Enquiry Skills Science Curriculum 2013

EYFS	Key Stage 1
• Show curiosity about objects, events and people (Playing and Exploring) • Question why things happen (Speaking: 30–50 months)	Explore the world around them and raise their own simple questions
• Engage in open-ended activity (Playing and Exploring)	Experience different types of science enquiries, including practical activities
• Take a risk, engage in new experiences and learn by trial and error (Playing and Exploring)	Begin to recognize different ways in which they might answer scientific questions
• Find ways to solve problems/find new ways to do things/test their ideas (Creating and Thinking Critically)	Carry out simple tests
• Develop ideas of grouping, sequences, cause and effect (Creating and Thinking Critically) • Know about similarities and differences in relation to places, objects, materials and living things (ELG: The World)	Use simple features to compare objects, materials and living things and, with help, decide how to sort and group them (Identifying and classifying)
• Comments and asks questions about aspects of their familiar world such as the place where they live or the natural world (The World: 30–50 months)	Ask people questions and use simple secondary sources to find answers
• Closely observes what animals, people and vehicles do (The World 8–20 months) • Use senses to explore the world around them (Playing and Exploring)	Observe closely using simple equipment With help, observe changes over time
• Make links and notice patterns in their experience (Creating and Thinking Critically)	With guidance, they should begin to notice patterns and relationships
• Choose the resources they need for their chosen activities (ELG: Self Confidence and Self Awareness) • Handle equipment and tools effectively (ELG: Moving and Handling)	Use simple measurements and equipment (e.g. hand lenses, egg timers) to gather data
• Create simple representations of events, people and objects (Being Imaginative: 40–60+ months)	Record simple data
• Answer how and why questions about their experiences (ELG: Understanding) • Make observations of animals and plants and explain why some things occur, and talk about changes (ELG: The World)	Use their observations and ideas to suggest answers to questions Talk about what they have found out and how they found it out
• Develop their own narratives and explanations by connecting ideas or events (ELG: Speaking) • Builds up vocabulary that reflects the breadth of their experience (Understanding: 30–50 months)	With help, they should record and communicate their findings in a range of ways and begin to use simple scientific language

Table 4.2 Working Scientifically: Pupils are not expected to cover each aspect for every area of study. Science Curriculum 2013

Key Stage 1	Lower Key Stage 2	Upper Key Stage 2
Explore the world around them and raise their own simple questions	Raise their own relevant questions about the world around them	Use their science experiences to explore ideas and raise different kinds of questions
Experience different types of science enquiries, including practical activities	Should be given a range of scientific experiences including different types of science enquiries to answer questions	Talk about how scientific ideas have developed over time
Begin to recognize different ways in which they might answer scientific questions	Start to make their own decisions about the most appropriate type of scientific enquiry they might use to answer questions	Select and plan the most appropriate type of scientific enquiry to use to answer scientific questions
Carry out simple tests	Set up simple practical enquiries, comparative and fair tests Recognize when a simple fair test is necessary and help to decide how to set it up	Recognize when and how to set up comparative and fair tests and explain which variables need to be controlled and why
Use simple features to compare objects, materials and living things and, with help, decide how to sort and group them (identifying and classifying)	Talk about criteria for grouping, sorting and classifying; and use simple keys	Use and develop keys and other information records to identify, classify and describe living things and materials, and identify patterns that might be found in the natural environment
Ask people questions and use simple secondary sources to find answers	Recognize when and how secondary sources might help them to answer questions that cannot be answered through practical investigations	Recognize which secondary sources will be most useful to research their ideas and begin to separate opinion from fact
Observe closely using simple equipment With help, observe changes over time	Make systematic and careful observations Help to make decisions about what observations to make, how long to make them for and the type of simple equipment that might be used	Make their own decisions about what observations to make, what measurements to use and how long to make them for
With guidance, they should begin to notice patterns and relationships	Begin to look for naturally occurring patterns and relationships and decide what data to collect to identify them	Look for different causal relationships in their data and identify evidence that refutes or supports their ideas
Use simple measurements and equipment (e.g. hand lenses, egg timers) to gather data	Take accurate measurements using standard units Learn how to use a range of (new) equipment, such as data loggers/thermometers appropriately	Choose the most appropriate equipment to make measurements with increasing precision and explain how to use it accurately. Take repeat measurements where appropriate.

Table 4.2 Continued

Key Stage 1	Lower Key Stage 2	Upper Key Stage 2
Record simple data	Collect and record data from their own observations and measurements in a variety of ways: notes, bar charts and tables, standard units, drawings, labelled diagrams, keys and help to make decisions about how to analyse this data	Decide how to record data and results of increasing complexity from a choice of familiar approaches: scientific diagrams and labels, classification keys, tables, scatter graphs, bar and line graphs
Use their observations and ideas to suggest answers to questions Talk about what they have found out and how they found it out	With help, pupils should look for changes, patterns, similarities and differences in their data in order to draw simple conclusions and answer questions.	Identify scientific evidence that has been used to support or refute ideas or arguments
With help, they should record and communicate their findings in a range of ways and begin to use simple scientific language	Use relevant simple scientific language to discuss their ideas and communicate their findings in ways that are appropriate for different audiences, including oral and written explanations, displays or presentations of results and conclusions	Use relevant scientific language and illustrations to discuss, communicate and justify their scientific ideas, Use oral and written forms such as displays and other presentations to report conclusions, causal relationships and explanations of degree of trust in results
	With support, they should identify new questions arising from the data, making predictions for new values within or beyond the data they have collected and finding ways of improving what they have already done.	Use their results to make predictions and identify when further observations, comparative and fair tests might be needed

It is difficult to imagine that these skills can develop at an acceptable rate and to the age-related expectations of the programmes of study without a rich and regular opportunity to engage in the skills and processes. Given that science is a core subject, one might wonder why in some schools the children only get an hour of science each week, or worse still, a science week once a year. In some schools, science is only taught every other half term.

Pause for thought

- How often is science taught to the children in your base class?
- Do you consider that the children get enough experience of science to develop their enquiry skills?
- How does the amount of time allocated to science compare with that allocated to maths or English?
- What are your thoughts on this provision?

How can using process skills develop children's autonomy?

As teachers, what we should be aiming for is independent learners who can raise questions and decide how to answer them, make decisions and consider whether results are valid. This is what working scientifically fosters. If children are allowed to explore and experience concrete resources, ideas that are relevant to their lives, and see the point of science, then they will develop their autonomy and their skills in analysing and evaluating, as well as their respect for evidence. This is metacognition.

> Teachers who showed pupils how they could ask their own questions and set up investigations that would help to reveal answers to those questions experimentally showed that this could be done well. (Ofsted 2013:11)

Parts A and B of this report refer to factors that were effective in promoting high achievement in the schools visited, namely:

- Accurate evaluation of science outcomes leading to effective improvement strategies
- Making science interesting
- Assessment for learning
- Effective differentiation
- Support for learning beyond lessons
- Time for learners to develop science practical skills

(Ofsted 2013)

So, by allowing children to explore; equipment, resources and ideas, we are encouraging them to be independent thinkers, who ask questions about the world around them. We need to challenge their thinking through our questioning, so that they see that questions are a good thing; they help us find answers. It is also important that we allow enough time in the curriculum allocation of finishing off their enquiries so that they feel satisfied that they have the autonomy to find the answers, or raise more questions.

It seems to us that another powerful way to help children to have autonomy is to help them see the relevance of science in their lives. Many children, as we have discussed, lose the curiosity to ask questions, and this may in part be because they don't think of science being part of their lives. If we can help them to see that science is all around, and will be useful to them, we have a better chance of keeping them engaged and developing that autonomy. By that we mean, that if they can see that it helps the car mechanic to do the job if they have an understanding of friction and lubrication, of levers, cogs and pulleys and how an internal combustion engine works (how *does* an internal engine get enough oxygen for combustion to occur?), then they will see science as a worthwhile endeavour.

Pause for thought

- What scientific concepts would it be worthwhile for children to know if they wanted to be a chef; a gardener; a nurse; a hairdresser?
- What about a builder?
- Can you make the links between working scientifically and any jobs or professions?

How does talk develop science enquiry skills and concepts?

According to de Jong et al. (2009), hands-on experiences, as well as discussion about what has been observed, listening to peers, and the scaffolding that comes from carefully thought-out questioning from adults, enhance children's questions about the world and help them to make better sense of the world. This fits neatly with the social-constructivist view of learning. Whereas Piaget saw children as constructing knowledge on their own, Vygotsky (1978) recognized the socio-cultural elements of learning, in particular through the interaction with a More Knowledgeable Other (MKO).

Talk, then, is a vital aspect of developing children's understanding, because if children are engaged with the talking, then they are reorganizing their thinking, which in turn leads to more transformative learning. That is learning that has transformed thinking and thus developed deeper understanding. When children are talking to each other they are explaining their ideas to each other. Besides, when children have different ideas about the science they are experience, they will challenge each other, and this helps them to make sense of the ideas (Mercer 1995). Furthermore, when children are talking to each other, they have to learn to listen carefully to each other and respond with further justification or explanations of their alternative 'sense-making'.

You could say then, that a quiet science classroom is one where not much learning is going on. Indeed, according to Ofsted (2013) they identified that where there were lower expectations and shaky confidence in subject knowledge among teachers;

> There was a strong tendency towards worksheets that, ostensibly, 'scaffolded' the activity but more frequently were preventing the pupils from thinking for themselves about the experimental method. (Ofsted 2013:14)

Not much talk going on in those classrooms, we suspect!

Another essential element of children talking about their science understandings is that as the teacher, we are able to listen to the children's ideas, and pick up on any misconceptions. Large research projects such as SPACE (Science, Processes and Concepts Exploration 1990–98) identified that children are remarkably similar about the ideas that children have about the world around them, despite many differing experiences and cultural backgrounds. This opportunity for Assessment for Learning (AfL) enables teachers to do their job of teaching effectively. From picking up the children's ideas, practitioners can guide children towards testing out their ideas and developing their understanding through a range of different enquiry, just as the example given in section 3. As reflective practitioners, it is very helpful to your science teaching for you to be aware of the many alternative ideas that children commonly hold and information about these is readily available in textbooks written for the purpose (Allen 2014; Rutledge 2010).

One important aspect about children talking in order to develop their scientific thinking is for the teacher to scaffold (Wood et al. 1988) the evaluation of the results and coming to conclusions about what the children now understand. How has their thinking changed in the light of the evidence that their enquiries provided? In many schools that we visit to support our PGCE students, there seems to be a policy of written evidence in the children's books. This is meant to be evidence of learning and teachers dutifully formatively mark the children's efforts, with next-step comments. We would argue that in the accountability culture of many schools today, the 'evidence in the books' is actually of teachers having delivered the curriculum, rather than evidence of learning. This will be explored further in the last chapter, but it is worth spending some time thinking about this.

Scientists do communicate their results to their colleagues in the scientific community, and they definitely do this through writing about their findings in journal articles, for example, so I am not suggesting that science writing is to be abandoned. However, scientists also communicate their findings through presenting to each other in conference, or through talking to a 'poster' of their research, and we believe that teachers would get to know much more about their children's learning through asking children to present to each other sometimes. Children can often articulate their understandings orally far in advance of what they explain in writing.

Alexander (2017) talks about dialogic teaching which uses the power of talking to extend thinking and promote understanding. This fits well with the social-constructivist view of learning (Vygotsky 1978a, b; Bruner 1966) that recognizes the importance of 'scaffolding' the learning through dialogue with the More Knowledgeable Other, which could be the teacher or peers.

Of course finding out about children's ideas, and encouraging them to talk, to you, as the teacher, or to their peers while you 'listen in', can only be done in a classroom where the ethos is one of talk. How can you encourage this kind of 'exploratory talk', which so supports children's deeper understanding (Mercer et al. 2004)? Work done by Naylor and Keogh (2000) has explored the use of 'concept cartoons', which give a picture of several children discussing a concept, and giving their opinion. Children in a group are encouraged to decide, by talking with each other, which of the children in the cartoon might be 'right', and to defend their views with explanations. Others in the group might challenge their ideas, and so some children may shift their thinking: transformational learning may occur. Naylor and Keogh (2006) went on to explore how large puppets in the classroom can be used to similar effect, if the puppet should give an alternative idea about the science being studied. Their research has shown that children are usually eager to respond to the puppet and to give their more reasoned, scientific explanation. In case you're thinking that the puppets would only be suitable for EYFS and KS1, Naylor and Keogh's (2006) research showed that the puppets facilitated more talk for learning even with 11-year-olds.

Summary

- What enquiry learning is in primary science?
- What is the role of practical activity in science?
- Why learning through enquiry is important?
- How talk develops science knowledge and understanding?
- How using the process of enquiry can develop children's autonomy?

Children are the research and development division of the human species. If they are permitted to do that research – to raise and explore their own questions through various forms of experimentation, and without being burdened with instructions – they exhibit signs of more creativity and curiosity. (Alison Gopnik)

Recommended reading

Centre for Industry Education Collaboration. Working Scientifically in the Primary Classroom: Progression of Enquiry Skills from EYFS to KS3. www.ciec.org.uk (accessed 11th November 2016)

Eley, A. (2016). How the 'I can explain!' project helps children learn science through talk. Primary Science No 142. Available at www.ase.org.uk

Harlen, W. (2010). *Principles and Big Ideas of Science Education*, Association for Science Education, Hatfield.

Hoath, L. (2008). Does 'Why' matter? Primary Science No 105. Available at www.ase.org.uk

Holligan, B. (2013). Giving children ownership of their science investigations is easier than you might think. *Primary Science No 128*. Available at www.ase.org.uk

Turner, J., Keogh, B., Naylor, S. and Lawrence, L. (2011). *It's Not Fair – or is it?* Millgate House Publishers, Sandbach and Association for Science Education, Hatfield.

Wesley, L. (2017). Add more gin! Common misconceptions and strategies for correcting them. Primary Science No 148. Available from www.ase.org.uk

Chapter 5
Skills to Develop in Science

A child who is protected from all controversial ideas is as vulnerable as a child who is protected from every germ. The infection, when it comes – and it will come – may overwhelm the system, be it the immune system or the belief system!

Jane Smiley

Chapter objectives

By the end of this chapter you will have developed an understanding of:

- What socioscientific issues are and how engaging in them is a pedagogical approach used to develop scientific conceptual understanding, scientific literacy and scientific enquiry skills;

- How socioscientific issues relate to the primary science curriculum, provide a rich context for children to work in and are a way to promote scientific understanding and engagement in science;

- Evolution and misconceptions that need to be considered by primary school teachers;

- Teaching strategies for delivering lessons focused on evolution;

- Teaching Sex and Relationships Education in primary schools – mandatory aspects relating to the science curriculum.

Introduction

In order not to repeat what has already been written in the preceding chapters, and to introduce the reader to wider aspects of science education which are engaging to primary-aged children, this chapter will focus on how scientific enquiry skills and understanding of science concepts can be developed by recognizing and examining socioscientific issues. Issues which primary teachers will, undoubtedly, encounter in the classroom and which children are highly interested in. This chapter will provide teaching strategies and ideas to enhance this pedagogical approach in the classroom. In addition, scientific misconceptions or alternative ideas are integral to a primary science teacher's pedagogy; being able to identify, challenge and reconstruct these both in the children that we teach and in ourselves is an important aspect of good practice in science teaching (Allen, 2014). Therefore, scientific misconceptions also known as children's alternative ideas will be discussed in relation to the topic of evolution, this being new to the Primary Science Curriculum in England and Wales – enabling trainee teachers to identify scientific misconceptions associated with evolution while also providing them with opportunities to select appropriate teaching strategies for providing lessons on evolution which is still, a topic, considered by some to be controversial. Finally, this chapter discusses the statutory requirements for delivering sex and relationships education (aspects of which fall under the statutory science curriculum), giving advice on how to deal appropriately and effectively with this area of the curriculum.

Curious children and how science provokes questions from children which can challenge us as teachers

Very early on in her teaching career, Amanda remembers a child in her year 2 (six years of age) class asking her the following: *'What is a clone and how can we make one?'* This particular child had been watching 'Star Wars' and wanted to know more. Amanda's first reaction was a huge smile – what a fantastic question – followed by the realization that this was not an uncomplicated area of science to explain simply, although at the time she did – never one to shy away from a challenge or indeed to dampen the enthusiasm of the children she has had the privilege to teach! This was the first of many socioscientific-related questions that Amanda would be asked throughout her teaching career.

   This sparked for Amanda, a research interest in how to teach primary-aged children about areas of science which might or might not be controversial in nature, which also develop the skills needed to become scientifically literate and which, ultimately, might affect our daily lives. Initial enquiries revealed that teaching socioscientific issues to primary-aged children was an under-researched area of science education, in fact almost non-existent. This has not been the case for KS3 and upwards (Sadler et al. 2016; Dawson and Venville, G. 2013; Kolsto 2006; Levinson 2006), which one would expect given the conceptual understanding needed to make decisions about some socioscientific issues. Nonetheless, this did not deter Amanda, instead it excited her to think that there was so much opportunity to research this area of science education. She was clearly not alone in thinking this as over the last ten years or so, some research has been undertaken and published in relation to the teaching of socioscientific issues in primary schools (Byrne et al. 2014; Dairianathan and Subramaniam 2011; Evagarou 2008); and this is something to celebrate; however, this still remains a severely under-researched area of science education.

What are socioscientific issues?

Socioscientific issues are multifaceted and controversial in nature; based in science, they have the potential to have a large impact on society. As we know, the society in which we live is embedded in an age of rapid social and technological change which might, or might not, have a positive impact on our lives.

> ### Pause for thought – *Thinking about the breadth of science*
>
> - Consider aspects which might be argued as 'controversial'.
> - How have you identified them? What makes them controversial?
> - Have any of these affected you personally?
> - Could any of these issues affect the children you teach or indeed be voiced by children in a primary classroom?
> - How will you address these issues? How does that make you feel as a science educator?

Let us take the example of the invention of mobile phones, which due to technological advances make them cheap and available to almost anyone who desires one. Mobile phones are convenient, can be used for a variety of tasks and have enabled parents to contact their children easily, helping them (and perhaps even their children) feel secure in the knowledge that they can contact their children wherever they are. We are of the generation that grew up without the constant distraction of a mobile phone or indeed the perception of it as a security blanket; we think we were fortunate. Not being in constant contact with our mothers or fathers from a young age enabled us to develop social independence, risk-taking skills (without the constant pressure that our children seem to be under from social media) and a relationship of trust with our parents or guardians. We find phone apps such as 'Phone Tracker' which uses a GPS tracking tool to allow the user to see the location of another smartphone user disconcerting to say the least; whether these apps are used by busy parents to keep tabs on their children, employers to know the whereabouts of employees or spouse's locating their husbands – it could be argued that used in this way, they are morally indefensible especially as there are now phone trackers which can track someone's location without the other party knowing about it! This is a perfect example of a socioscientific issue which could easily be discussed in the primary classroom, a forum for children to explore the social and moral implications of behaviours in which, they themselves, are engaged.

We are sure that anyone who knows a child with a mobile phone will agree that for a child, their mobile phone is almost like 'a part of them – a third limb'; it being challenging to separate the two! The fact that many mobile phones now easily connect to the internet can be positive if the internet is being used to research school work or further understanding; however, access to the internet also presents in itself numerous issues; an unhealthy, constant obsession with mobile phones, or indeed online social media, can adversely affect children's social skills and self-esteem; excessive access to social media can create anxieties in children and add even more pressure to conform to so-called societal norms.

The Office for National Statistics (ONS 2015) found that although social media may *'provide an additional way to connect with others and form relationships'*, unfortunately, they are a potential vehicle for *'social comparison, cyber bullying and isolation'*. This can also have a negative impact on a child's mental health with the same report arguing that 27 per cent of children (10–15-year-olds) who spend three or more hours a day on social media websites display symptoms of mental ill-health (data from the report was compared with data from the Strengths and Difficulties Questionnaire Score – a measure of mental illness) compared with 12 per cent of children who spend no time on social networking websites. This percentage decreases to 11 per cent for those children who spend less than three hours per day on social media.

Worryingly, more and more children are being exposed to pornographic images (via their own exploration of the internet) and sexting (transmitting sexual images via their mobile phone – whether consensually, coercively or non-consensually) and it might, or might not, surprise you to know that this is now becoming more frequent for primary-aged pupils. A failure to tackle the influence of pornography can leave pupils open to exploitation as they grow up (Ofsted 2013) and with a distorted view of what is normal – both in terms of body image and sexual relationships (PHSE Association 2012). Furthermore, a porn culture can, in particular, leave girls at primary school facing sexist abuse (Women and Equalities Committee 2016); therefore, it is now more likely that as a primary classroom practitioner you will be confronted with instances of this. How equipped do you feel to deal with this? We will return to this further on in the chapter when we discuss sex and relationships education.

Therefore, it is clear to see that the controversial issues of contemporary life are issues about which there might very well be social disagreement (different individuals and groups interpret and understand in differing ways), competition or conflict but are not easy to define (Sadler et al. 2016; Woolley 2010; Levinson 2006). It may be an issue for which society has not found a solution that can be almost universally accepted or one which has sufficient significance that each of the proposed ways in dealing with it is objectionable to some section of the community and arouses dissent, opposition or protest. It is also crucial to understand that a *'controversial issue must involve value judgements, so that the issue cannot be settled by facts, evidence or experiment alone'* (Wellington 1986: 3). Therefore, socioscientific issues are as follows:

- *Controversial*;
- Involve *values*;
- Require *ethical reasoning* (as well as scientific reasoning) about a vast range of scientific topics.

Why use socioscientific issues as a pedagogy to teach primary science?

Engagement and pupil motivation

You might feel that as a primary science teacher, socioscientific issues are not and will not be a consideration or an issue for you in your primary classroom; ***however, nothing could be further from the truth***. One of the most important aspects of teaching is pupil motivation and engagement in contemporary issues is what stimulates most interest from students (Sadler 2011; Claire and Holden 2007). If the social and ethical aspects of science were included more fully in school science then many pupils may be encouraged to study science longer, as the humanistic side of science appeals to many pupils, particularly girls and it is crucial for us to enable girls to see that science and maths is '*for them*' if we want to close the gender gap when it comes to studying maths and the sciences at higher levels and thus, access to a wide range of rewarding careers; although there has been an improvement in this area, there is still a very long way to go (CFE, 2017 found that the 30 per cent of primary-aged girls considering a career in science leaned towards careers in the biological sciences); especially when we consider that only 28 per cent of the world's researchers are women (Reuters 2016)! As we know, children start to develop a love for science in the primary school which can only happen if primary-aged children experience inspiring science that '*builds their understanding of the value and place of science in their lives*' (Wellcome Trust 2013: 4).

The changes that have come into play in the national curriculum for primary science (2013) have had both its critics and advocates and we, as science educators, are both depending on which aspect of the curriculum is being discussed. However, one aspect of the curriculum, which we think is fantastic, is the emphasis on scientific enquiry and thinking skills – the breadth of which has been thoroughly discussed in Chapter 4 – and the aims that children are given opportunities to:

- *develop understanding of the nature, processes and methods of science through different types of science enquiries **that help them to answer scientific questions about the world around them***;
- *become equipped with the scientific knowledge required to understand the uses and **implications of science, today and for the future** [and]*,

- *understand the importance that science holds **in their everyday lives and people in general*** (DfE 2013: 3).

Interestingly, guidance for the national curriculum also states that the social and economic implications of science are taught most appropriately within the wider school curriculum, which I would interpret as a recognition of the strength of primary teaching – taking a cross-curricular approach to teaching and learning. It is important to remember that science and society are not separate independent entities but rather all aspects of science are inseparable from the society from which they arise. Indeed, being able to identify the ethical implications for our actions as individuals and as a society, regardless of the context, is imperative if we are to avoid repeating past disasters such as Chernobyl and, as importantly, if we are to give a forum to the voices '*of those likely to be most affected – disabled people, ethnic groups, women, people with genetic conditions, gays and lesbians, those unable to have children – who are too rarely heard*' (Levinson and Reiss 2003: 3).

To us, this is significant, not simply as an educator **but more importantly as members of the human race***. Throughout our lives, we are faced with choices about a whole range of issues; engaging in debate about ethical issues gives children the opportunity to develop their skills of reasoned argument necessary for making possible choices; a huge part of this is being able to think and reason scientifically. We *passionately* believe that this does not begin in a child's secondary school career! *It is **imperative*** for primary school teachers to educate children from a young age to develop their understanding of scientific knowledge and use this and scientific evidence to inform their scientific thinking so that they can express their view and participate in making decisions about issues that they are passionate about or that might very well affect them, either now or in the future.

Therefore, in primary science education, we believe (and hope) that we really are at an exciting precipice of change. The national curriculum actively encourages creativity, '*teachers will wish to use different contexts to maximise their pupils' engagement with and motivation to study science*' (DfE 2013: 3) which Wyse and Dowson (2009) argue is a right not a privilege. This gives primary schools the freedom to deliver the curriculum in ways which they see best; as long as the statutory requirements are included and children are given both the opportunities and time to develop their enquiry skills.

It is our experience, that primary-aged children care deeply about the world they live in; children are naturally curious and it is the art of the teacher to not only elicit that curiosity but to also maintain it in the primary science classroom (Ofsted 2013a) which can be a challenge, especially as children can find some aspects of conceptual science difficult to understand because of their abstract nature (forces for example) or because of the nature of some scientific concepts being counter-intuitive (Loxley and Dawes 2013). This coupled with a relentless exposure to all aspects of science via a multitude of media; children will surprise you with the science-based questions that they ask you and you should be prepared that you *might not know* the answers to all they ask or indeed the pedagogical approaches to teach them! This is often an anxiety for those teaching primary science and we are not simply referring to student teachers. As we have clearly argued in Chapter 2, there has been a history of underinvestment in primary science, especially in relation to the professional development of teachers, resources and access to science expertise (Wellcome Trust 2013); this does need to change but let us not make this an excuse for not teaching primary science in a way which enthrals and engages primary-aged children! All primary teachers need to be is creative and disciplined in their approaches to teaching and assessing primary science, using research-based evidence where they can.

Scientific literacy, argument and enquiry skills

In Chapter 1, we discussed scientific literacy as an important aim for science education; one of the aims of school science is to sharpen these skills as scientific literacy is a lifelong pursuit, engaging with socioscientific issues effectively will indeed aid this. The ability to understand and practise valid ways of arguing in a scientific context is an important aspect of scientific literacy; furthermore, teaching socioscientific issues develops students' willingness to reflect critically on their own knowledge and values. From a broader sociological perspective, there is a need to improve the quality of young people's understanding of the nature of scientific argument within the context of a society where scientific issues increasingly dominate. Children need to be able to recognize not only the strengths but also the limitations of such arguments.

Another way to achieve this is via argumentation (Simon et al. 2012) which enables children to take stances which they justify using evidence, and to evaluate evidence that is used to either support or refute different scientific claims. This gives children opportunities to have a clearer understanding of the nature of scientific enquiry and the ways in which scientists' work – this being another aim of the national curriculum for science (2013).

Learning these skills has a cross-curricular educational value as they can be applied more widely. Ultimately, structured arguments in science lessons can reveal scientific misconceptions, stimulate pupil thinking, have a positive impact on pupil engagement and motivation, promote inclusion and encourage an environment where learning together is *valued* and that arguments and opinions are valued (Allen 2014; Simon et al. 2012; Shakespeare 2003).

Why is this important? Historically children have needed a forum to discuss issues which have affected them; for example, illnesses such as cancer, and, as science and technology has rapidly changed in recent years throwing up all sorts of issues, so has the children's need to discuss them; schools need to provide a forum for this, especially as this might very well not be provided at home. As Woolley rightly argues:

> Children are facing difficult issues every day. … They are concerned about how they can be listened to and really heard. They are also interested in how they can make a difference and get involved. To ignore this experience and such interests/concerns is to try and educate a child without considering who they really are. (2010: 16)

There is now much more support for primary classroom practitioners to use these pedagogical approaches in their classroom; for example, the overarching aim of the PARRISE project (www.parrise.eu) is to share and improve best practices integrating the pedagogical approaches discussed in this chapter: inquiry-based science education (IBSE) and learning based on socioscientific issues. The researchers call their innovative approach Socio-Scientific Inquiry-Based Learning (SSIBL) which scaffolds pedagogy so that teachers can build confidence together as they develop the skills needed to teach science in this way. The Primary Science Teaching Trust (PSTT; www.pstt.org.uk) offers primary teachers' continual professional development for teaching argumentation in school science and the Association of Science Education (ASE; www.ase.org.uk) provides teaching resources and advice on how to incorporate this pedagogical approach to teaching science.

Socioscientific issues and the primary science National Curriculum

There is so much scope for incorporating socioscientific issues into your teaching; before reading the next section please consider the questions in the following pause for thought.

Table 5.1 Areas of the primary science national curriculum which could pertain to socioscientific issues

Biology	Chemistry	Physics
• Animals, including humans	• Acid rain	• Electric cars and energy consumption
• Biodiversity – eco systems and habitats	• Environmental issues: the weather – flooding for example	• Nuclear power
• Drugs – using drugs in sport	• Energy efficiency	• Qualifying characteristics of a planet (what makes a planet a planet – Pluto for example)
• Endangered Species	• Fossil fuels	
• Evolution and Inheritance	• Global warming	
• Food	• Sustainability linked to materials	• Renewable energies (solar/wind) and cost
• Health		
• Nutrition	• Mining and quarrying	• Space exploration (search for life) and cost
• Sustainability (fishing)	• Oil spills	
• Vaccinations	• Pollution	• Technology – mobile phones
• Zoos	• Recycling	• The age of the universe/Earth

Pause for thought – *Animals in captivity*

- What questions can you think of that are related to this area of science which might include controversial issues?
- Which questions are suitable to discuss with primary-aged children?
- Which areas of the curriculum do they refer to?
- Which enquiry skills (process skills) will the children be using when discussing them?
- What evidence will the children need to understand and use to justify their arguments?

Figure 5.1 An example of how to incorporate socioscientific issues – is it right to keep killer whales in captivity? Paired work by two year 6 children using scientific research enquiry skills, ICT, reasoning based on scientific evidence and moral considerations, plus drawings to present their work

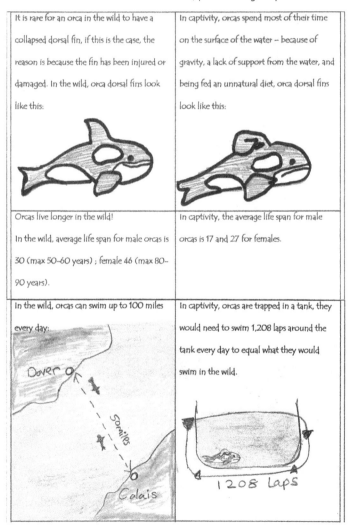

Figure 5.1 Continued

In the wild, there has only every been one reliable report of an orca harming a human.	In captivity, orcas have attacked and killed 3 humans since 1991 and injured many others because of the stress of being derpived a natural life.
In the wild, orcas are highly social animals, living in pods from 2 – 15, calves are raised by the pod . In some pods, calves stay with their mothers for life.	In captivity, orcas are forced to live with orcas from other pods, are moved between facilties for breeding and to perform. Tilikum, was snatched from his mother when he was just 2 years old – taken form his family, he was kept in a holding tank for almost a year before being transferred to a marine park.

Is it right to keep killer whales in captivity?

We think that it is very wrong to keep killer whales in captivity because –

- They are kept from their natural habitat, their dosral fins collapse
- They are kept away from their families, this is awful – this makes them very unhappy
- They don't live as long
- They become stressed and aggressive by being trapped
- It is wicked to keep them in such a small space when they are used to swimming for miles in oceans, they gnaw on the iron bars and concrete from being so stressed – this shows how much they want to escape, so would we if we were trapped and taken away from our family
- They are fed an unnatural diet – they are unable to hunt or obtain water from their prey
- Being in captivity is the same as being in prison but they have done nothing wrong
- They are not for our entertainment

Teaching socioscientific issues – what do teachers need to consider?

- Teachers and the children taking part need to understand the nature of the controversy – why, and in what ways, is this topic controversial (Oulton, Dillon and Grace 2004);
- Debate and discussion are key aspects of lessons based in socioscientific issues and ground rules need to be agreed for group work and debates (an important aspect of this is using scientific evidence to justify arguments

as well as being able to identify evidence that is irrelevant); as with any form of discussion and debate children need to be aware of the learning objective and their steps to success to meet the learning outcomes.

- Children must be given opportunities to also consider and think about the moral aspects of the issue using the language of morals, they will need practice to develop this skill; by considering problems with moral dimensions, children will start to acquire the language needed in order to articulate their ideas in a clear way.

- As one would expect, teachers should consider the cognitive capabilities of the children they are teaching in relation to the learning of the conceptual science.

- Teachers should provide opportunities for children to consider the local, national or global implications of the issue and, where appropriate, build on the interests of the child – children may be made aware of socioscientific issues via the media, movies, television and books and these can be a great starting point; however, teachers should provide children with opportunities to consider authentic socioscientific issues (Sadler, Romine and Topçu 2016; Levinson 2006), for example, how increased demand for food has meant that a change in traditional agricultural practices have changed, reducing the abundance of wildflowers in the English countryside and therefore, having a negative impact on the population of bumble bees.

- Pupils should not be pressed to agree on a final answer, solution or right answer; they need time to reflect and think; one way to do this is to look at the class coming to a consensus but pressure should not be put on children to conform to that consensus.

- Pupils should be encouraged to express their own views in a safe environment where they know that their *views are valued.*

- Children should be taught to appreciate the process, to take part in debate and discussion using scientific evidence (from a variety of sources) and language to support or refute arguments, they need to get used to there being uncertainty and not having a final right answer at the end thus developing a Growth Mindset (Dweck et al. 2012) which, not coincidentally, is also needed to develop the skills for maths mastery (Askew 2015).

- Teaching strategies are varied and can include group work or paired work, role-play such as decision alley or theatre, ICT, debates, producing information posters, PowerPoint presentations, assemblies and research activities (which incorporates a whole range of scientific enquiry skills); this also provides a wealth of cross-curricular links integral to primary education and beyond. Using a variety of teaching strategies also serves to ensure that children did not become **bored** with the work that they were undertaking, allowing them to be creative and express themselves in many different ways.

- Teaching socioscientific issues also enables strong links to English (newspaper reports, balanced arguments, scientific non-chronological reports, information texts, explanation texts, letter writing, biographies) and maths (data collection and representation, examining populations, arithmetic, geometry, pattern seeking, relationships between data; making quantitative measurements).

● Relating science to personally relevant contexts is a well-known strategy for making science and socioscientific issues accessible to students (Duschl et al. 2007; Kali et al. 2008).

● Where possible, teachers should plan opportunities for 'authentic' inquiry into socioscientific issues which reflect the real world, which come from the children themselves (this will need scaffolding) and which also enable children to improve their conceptual understanding of science topics (Sadler et al. 2016); for example, endangered species, recycling, flooding. One way to achieve this is via field trips which typically have a favourable impact not only on enhancing the children's learning, but also by further capturing the children's attention – therefore, adding to the authenticity of what the children are learning. Tal et al. (2011) observed that field trips enhanced group discourse, elicited a high degree of interest and engagement in genetics, by the students who took part in their study. It also provided the students with an opportunity for meaningful learning; Evagarou (2008) also found that a field trip – in this case a visit to a local pig farm by children aged 10–11 – had a positive impact on the students' motivation in engaging with socioscientific issues and furthering their understanding of the underlying scientific concepts.

● Inclusion will be addressed (and discussed in depth in Chapter 6); assessment will be varied (and discussed in depth in Chapter 7).

Possible challenges teachers need to consider when using this pedagogy

● Are the controversial aspects of the issue appropriate for the age of the children you are teaching and do you understand them?

● Before teaching in this way, engage with parents and let them know what you will be focusing on and why (include this pedagogy for science education in your school science policy).

● Might there be questions asked which are inappropriate and if so how will you address these?

● Time – these skills take time to develop and need; therefore, to be appropriately planned for, underpinned by conceptual science and process skills, and assessed.

● Teacher assessment must be valued; the obsession that some schools have with written evidence in books will not suffice to assess the scientific knowledge and skills learnt via this pedagogy!

Teaching in this way takes thoughtful planning, time and effort as well as an appreciation of a variety of teaching strategies, inclusion, social constructivism and assessment procedures (to which I return in Chapter 8) on the part of the teacher; taking risks and being reflective practitioners is how we become more effective teachers and avoid monotony and disengagement in our classrooms. No-one is suggesting that this happens overnight, this is a process that has rich outcomes!

Scientific misconceptions/children's alternative ideas – teaching about inheritance and evolution

New to the primary science curriculum (2013), some might argue that teaching about inheritance and the 'Theory of Evolution' can be challenging especially as it is a topic, considered by some, to be controversial; it is this perception that can make student teachers anxious when teaching this topic. However, we argue that this need not be the case; student teachers equipped with the correct subject knowledge and teaching pedagogies have nothing to fear. Therefore, what do student teachers need to consider when teaching this topic?

Let's start by examining the word *theory*! One of the important aims of science education is to teach children to correctly use and understand the scientific meaning of vocabulary. In everyday life, we might consider the word *theory* to mean:

- A guess;
- An idea based on experience;
- A hunch with little evidence or support.

However, in science, a theory means an explanation, underpinned by robust evidence, to explain phenomena. A scientific theory must be strongly supported by many different lines of evidence in order to be accepted by the scientific community. The incorrect, lay-definition of 'theory' used in everyday life has been utilized by some, to criticize the Theory of Evolution by emphasizing that scientific theories are not absolute or additionally presents it, incorrectly and misleadingly, as a matter of opinion rather than based in scientific evidence. Some might argue that it is therefore not helpful to use the word theory when referring to evolution as this can lead to confusion and thus it is a good idea to omit or avoid the use of the word (Harlock et al. 2015); however, we would disagree with this. Indeed, the science programmes of study for KS2 do not include the word 'theory' in its statutory guidance in relation to evolution but interestingly does so for the theory of gravitation (DfE 2013: 30) which can be argued communicates a conflicting message. There are many instances in the primary science curriculum where language has a dual or even multiple meaning; children must learn to understand

and use the scientific meaning of vocabulary. Including the word theory in relation to evolution is a perfect opportunity to:

- *enable pupils to develop a deeper understanding of a wide range of scientific ideas;*
- *begin to recognise, and talk about how, scientific ideas change and develop over time;*
- *use relevant scientific language to communicate and justify their scientific ideas* (DfE 2013: 24).

Furthermore, it gives children opportunities to develop an understanding of what real science is and what real scientists do in order to deepen their understanding of the scientific process. We must remember that there are still strong arguments that school science bears only a partial resemblance to real science, with too much emphasis being placed on the learning of individual facts, hence the focus now on working scientifically. Facts – scientific knowledge – are part of science but they must not be confused with understanding. If teaching is fact-dominated then it leads to the view that science is capable of yielding ultimate truths, being value-free and simply 'proving' things. However, if science is seen as exploring ideas then the teaching will involve learners *in the process of developing understanding from evidence*; thus, developing scientific enquiry skills and thinking skills: *'Ideas will be explored rather than accepted and committed to memory. Alternative views will be examined in terms of supporting evidence'* (Harlen and Qualter 2014). This is important because as primary practitioners, we risk exposing our pupils to *'insecure, or superficial understanding [that] will not allow genuine progression; pupils may struggle at key points of transition (such as between primary and secondary school), [or] build up serious misconceptions'* (DfE 2013: 3).

The Theory of Evolution is a widely supported and overwhelming accepted scientific theory in the scientific community, what evidence exists to support it and what evidence is suitable to use with primary-aged children?

Evidence to support the Theory of Evolution (those highlighted in bold are suitable for teaching primary-aged children)

- Biochemistry – the biochemistry of living things on earth is incredibly similar demonstrating that certain organisms share a common ancestry
- Biogeography – the study of living things around the globe, biogeographers compare the distribution of organisms living today or those that lived in

the past (fossils); findings indicate that species are distributed across the earth in a pattern that reflects their genetic relationship to one another and demonstrates that related organisms derive from the same common ancestor

- **Classification and inheritance**
- **Comparative anatomy – the comparison of the structures of different living things**
- Comparative embryology – comparing the embryos of different organisms
- **Fossil evidence and Palaeontology – the study of prehistoric life via fossil evidence**
- Genetics – DNA, inheritance
- **Measurements of evolutionary changes in the population of organisms alive today, evolution in action, for example, antibiotic-resistant bacteria; or fast-changing viruses such as influenza**
- Molecular biology – gene sequences, for example

The following are examples of how some of the above can be utilized in the primary classroom.

a) Comparative anatomy – pentadactyl limbs

Primary-aged children are required to learn about the human skeleton and its uses in lower KS2. Building on this, an interesting and exciting way to learn about evolution and common ancestry would be by teaching children about comparative anatomy in vertebrates. One simple way to achieve this could be for children to examine the similarities between humans and other members of the ape superfamily; giving

Figure 5.2 Skeletons of members of the ape superfamily (with thanks to UCL Grant Museum)

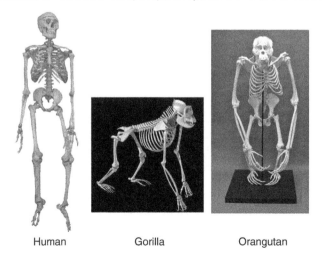

Human   Gorilla   Orangutan

reasons for classifying these as greater apes based on specific characteristics that the animals have in common.

> ## Pause for thought
>
> - What similarities and differences can you see in Figure 5.3?
> - Can you account for these using your knowledge and understanding of evolution?

Figure 5.3 is an example of homologous structures in vertebrates, pentadactyl limbs which have five digits – thus, the same bones (because they are inherited from a common ancestor) but specialized for different functions. The pentadactyl limbs cannot be seen without examining the skeleton of the animals, but once studied using scientific enquiry skills (observation, questioning, recording, pattern seeking, using evidence to explain scientifically), children can understand how different species within a classified group are related and learn about how scientific evidence suggests that vertebrates descend from one common ancestor. This incorporates another area of the primary science curriculum – examining fossils; children can be given the opportunity to discuss and examine 'fossil records' to show compare and contrast modern animals with their ancestors. This also gives primary-aged children opportunities to give priority to and formulate explanations from evidence (DfE 2013; Levy et al. 2011).

Figure 5.3 The pentadactyl forelimb of a bat, cat, human and whale

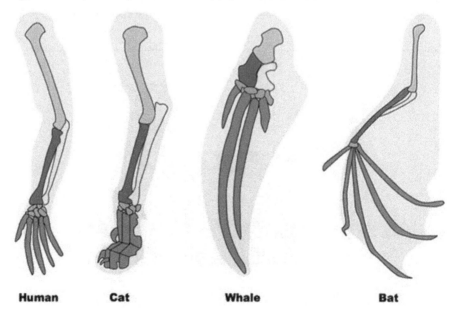

Human   Cat   Whale   Bat

Figure 5.4 The evolution of modern-day toothed whale according to fossil evidence

D. *Dorudon* (Basilosauridae) from the middle to late Eocene of Egypt

1 Present – modern toothed whales

C. *Rodhocetus* (Protocetidae) from the early middle Eocene of Pakistan

2 Thirty million years ago – rodhocetus kasrani, reduced hind limbs could have aided in swimming; it swam with an up and down motion just like modern-day whales

B. *Pakicetus* (Pakicetidae) from the earliest middle Eocene of Pakistan

3 Forty-five million years ago – ambulocetus natans, probably walked on land but also swam by paddling with its hind legs

A. *Elomeryx* (Anthracotheriidae) from the Oligocene of Europe, North America, Asia

4 Sixty million years ago – hypothetical mesonychid skeleton.

For example, a whale is a placental mammal as are humans; and many other mammals – and all placental mammals share a common ancestor. From examining fossils, scientists argue that the first whales were in fact land animals with pentadactyl limbs, the limbs being important for daily life moving around the land. The skeleton of a modern-day whale, which lives its life in the water, still has the pentadactyl limbs but they are now used differently (this is clearly illustrated via the blue whale currently suspended beautifully in the Hintz Hall at the Natural History Museum) – it has a collection of bones in its flippers (which closely corresponds to the bones in the human arm and hand). This enables children to understand that living things, in this case vertebrates, share anatomical characteristics which have changed over time (DfE 2013) due to evolution.

Children can easily access photographs, interactive films and scientific drawings to examine via the internet or scientific books for an activity based on pentadactyl limbs; they can draw their observations or indeed make a model, as in Figure 5.5, as well as being highlighted in the KS2 programmes of study. However, examining and making observations of real limbs is much more exciting. Many museums offer workshops for children to examine skeletons and specimens, both at the museum and via outreach workshops using fossils, specimens and bones; for example, UCL's Grant Museum of Zoology houses around 68,000 zoological specimens with many of the species endangered or extinct, the dodo for example. They offer a range of

Figure 5.5 The pentadactyl limb of a bat represented via a model. This child has used play dough to create her model

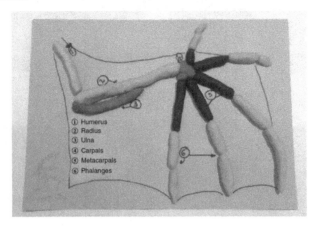

exciting educational workshops focused on adaptations and evolution, bones and skeletons, classification and grouping, teeth, eating and diet and furthermore, you can choose which specimens you would like to examine during your workshop! Interaction between the museum staff and your pupils *'is a powerful tool to support pupils' learning of concepts as well as development of enquiry skills'* (Veall 2015: 77).

Teachers could ask their pupils to firstly make systematic and careful observations about pentadactyl limb bones, drawing the limb bones and encouraging their pupils to see and explain any patterns that exist (pattern seeking); for example, the pentadactyl bone pattern. They could also represent their observations as models (a representation of an idea, object, process or system) as in Figure 5.5, which is of course central to what scientists do when researching and communicating their findings (DfE 2013). Then, by examining the pentadactyl limbs of a human and whale, pupils should be encouraged to explain the differences between the two in light of the environment in which the animal lives (identifying how animals are adapted to suit their environment). Challenging pupils further, teachers could then ask pupils to predict what other animals might have pentadactyl limbs using their understanding of the Theory of Evolution, or indeed teachers could provide opportunities for children to examine and classify a specimen unknown to the children.

As already stated, curiosity in children is a key principle in teaching science; *'the best teachers of science set out to first maintain curiosity in their pupils'* (Ofsted 2013b: 4) and this activity is an example of this. Examining the skeletons of these can come after pupils have examined other aspects of the animals such as physical features of the body, lifecycles, diet, habitats, how nutrients and water are transported within the animals (year 6 programme of study, 2015). This builds on the learning that children would have done in KS1 about animals including humans where children have compared and contrasted animals at first-hand. The fact that humans are part of the animal kingdom can be difficult for some children to understand or even accept; this activity gives children an opportunity to deepen their understanding of classification via examining evolution and reconstruct any scientific misconceptions.

b) Adaptations, inheritance – variation between individuals of the same species: Darwin's finches

Darwin's five-year voyage on the Beagle is an ideal setting for an activity on variation. During his voyage of scientific discovery, Darwin visited the Galapagos Islands; he used his scientific observations, in this case the distribution of finches across the islands, to formulate his Theory of Evolution by natural selection which states that there is variation between individuals of the same species. Characteristics which give individuals a better chance of survival and reproduction in their environment are advantageous; these characteristics will then be passed on to the next generation and thus become more common as a result.

By studying the beaks of different finches and their food sources (on different islands), children are encouraged to explain what is different about the beaks of the finches on the different islands (size and shape – variation) and why (because they have evolved to feed on the food sources of the island on which they inhabited – adaptation and inheritance). To extend this, children could then be given time to predict other habitats that each finch could survive in and why (or why not) using their scientific research skills and explanations. Using the differences in the beaks of finches as a way to learn about adaptation, inheritance and variation can also enable children to learn about the process of scientific discovery that Darwin undertook – setting this in an historical context.

Challenges in teaching inheritance and the Theory of Evolution – is this a controversial subject?

One of the principle concerns that some teachers and student teachers have about teaching the Theory of Evolution is what, they initially see, as a conflict between science and religion; it is this, that for some make this topic controversial. Despite the ever-growing mountain of evidence, many people still do not accept evolution as the best explanation for the development of life on Earth as some people believe that it conflicts with their religious beliefs or that it is improbable, life being too complex to have arisen by chance.

On the other hand, there are many religious people who accept that evolution occurs as described by biologists, but under the direction of God (theistic evolution). For example, Frances Collins is an American geneticist who is also a Christian. He notes that he sees no conflict in what the Christian Bible tells him about God and what science tells him about nature.

CASE STUDY 5.1

I do not find the wording of Genesis 1 and 2 to suggest a scientific textbook but a powerful and poetic description of God's intentions in creating the universe. The mechanism of creation is left unspecified. If God, who is all powerful and who is not limited by space and time, chose to use the mechanism of evolution to create you and me, who are we to say that wasn't an absolutely elegant plan? And if God has now given us the intelligence and the opportunity to discover his methods, that is something to celebrate (Van Biema 2005: 1).

Therefore, evolution should be taught that it is a scientific theory, based on robust scientific evidence which explains how organisms change and adapt over a period of time *and certainly not as an alternative to religion.* Evolution makes no statements about the existence of God and neither should classroom teachers.

CASE STUDY 5.2

Student X discusses her experiences of teaching evolution in year 6.

'Oh my goodness what an experience! The school decided to teach 7 hours of it during SATS week. Bit of light relief for the children! Previous year they had apparently used lesson plans from X … . which look like GCSE level to me. I planned a time line activity as an introduction (Montessori idea). One child asked if that meant a human could give birth to a guinea pig! Several more commented that their God had made us all a certain fixed way. Two weeks later I had to get the headmistress involved as they would not consider what I was teaching due to some of their religious beliefs – one child told me his Dad wanted to have a word with me to put me straight. She was great, told the children they had to open-up their minds and understand things even if they decided to disagree. It made a real difference. What a tough subject to teach! Intellectually as well as morally. Had to make lots of games – finches beaks as you suggested. Your horse fossil sketches really helped and your beetle slides. And several teachers told the children they were descended from monkeys – glad you highlighted that misconception!'

Pause for thought

- What are your reflections about both case studies 5.1 and 5.2?
- Do you agree? Disagree?
- Does any of this have a place in the primary classroom?
- How would you deal with what has been described in case study 5.2?
- How prepared do you feel to teach evolution?
- Where can you seek guidance and support for teaching evolution in school?

For our minds, there are a number of lessons to be learnt from the incident in case study 5.2:

1 School science policy and parental involvement; had this been updated to include the new curriculum? If so, how was this information disseminated to the parents? Was there a meeting? Were letters sent out to parents to explain the change of science policy? It might be the case that most of the parents were very well informed but for some, issues existed for them in their children learning about evolution. Therefore, how can schools inform parents scientific aims for this topic and stress that children and teachers are not taking part in theological arguments about religion or the existence of God? we would argue that it is worth either having a school meeting which informs parents of the changes to the curriculum and how the topic of evolution is to be taught, this would give parents the opportunity to discuss this in an open forum. It is worth noting that parents cannot remove their children from the statutory science curriculum and therefore a meeting with parents is not about gaining parental consent, but instead an opportunity for parents and staff to be clear on the learning aims and intentions of teaching evolution. This would have the dual effect of relaying any fears that parents might have as well as not putting teachers in vulnerable positions with parents.

2 Subject knowledge of teachers – it does not seem that certain teachers were clear on the scientific content knowledge of this area of the biology curriculum. Schools need to ensure that teachers have the necessary training to enhance their own subject knowledge about evolution and the development of pedagogical skills to teach this subject which includes an awareness of the possible controversies of this subject.

3 Teaching resources available to teach evolution, this topic is still relatively new to the curriculum but teaching resources are slowly starting to emerge. A good example of this is, 'Let's talk about Evolution' by Horlock, Naylor and Moules (2015), which includes an array of lesson ideas to teach evolution via enquiry. As the science curriculum states, conceptual scientific knowledge should be taught via scientific enquiry and therefore, schools and teachers must also ensure that they have a clear understanding of the breadth of scientific enquiry and how this can be taught effectively to enable children to deepen their conceptual understanding of science.

4 Misconceptions/alternative ideas about evolution are clearly present, can you identify them? The following are common misconceptions about evolution that primary school teachers and student teachers need to be aware of and understand.

Scientific misconceptions and evolution:

a) **'Survival of the fittest' or the 'fit enough'?**

Organisms do not need to be optimally adapted to survive – perfection does not exist; instead, organisms need to be 'fit enough to survive' in the habitat in which they live. If the environment changes however, a 'fit' organism's adaptation may no longer be successful and this will affect the organisms' ability to survive and reproduce; thus, affecting the survival of the species.

> It is not the strongest species that survive, nor the most intelligent, but the ones most responsive to change.
> - Charles Darwin

b) **The use of the word 'random'.**

Mutations in organisms do occur randomly; however, selection of these mutations is not random. Traits which are the most advantageous for the survival of the organism are selected for by the environmental conditions; therefore, if the environment changes drastically (think here of what is happening to the habitats of polar bears) then this might very well affect the survival chances of the species.

c) **An organism consciously chooses an adaptation or tries to adapt is incorrect.**

There is no plan or choice made by the organism to adapt; for example, the giraffe did not make a conscious decision to grow its neck longer so it was better adapted to its environment. The process of natural selection leads to some members of a species to survive or reproduce better depending on the characteristics they have. It is important here for children to understand that evolution happens over a long period of time and not within the life of one organism.

d) **Humans are evolved from monkeys – this is incorrect.**

Humans and monkeys share a common but very distant ancestor (many millions of years ago) – humans have not evolved from monkeys. Humans and monkeys are both classified as primates; however, humans belong to the superfamily of Hominoidea (Great Apes), genus (Homo).

e) **Humans co-existed with dinosaurs – this is incorrect.**

This is a common misconception due to movies, for example *One Million Years B.C.*, and cartoons, for example, the *Flintstones*. Dinosaurs became extinct 65 million years before humans came into existence.

Figure 5.6 Illustrates the point regarding adaptation well

By understanding what possible scientific misconceptions relate to the topic, student teachers can not only ensure that their own subject knowledge is sound but also identify misconceptions when they arise – possibly using them formatively to elicit children's ideas or indeed to reconstruct misconceptions during science lessons, although that is it important to note that children's ideas can be tenaciously held and take time to change (Allen 2014); nonetheless, it is the responsibility of the teacher of science to address these.

Provision for relationships and sex education

For the final part of this chapter, we now return to another area of the science curriculum which often creates anxiety and can be seen by some as controversial – relationships and sex education. Highly topical, fiercely debated and seldom out of the media – relationships and sex education has both its supporters and critics. The current RSE curriculum (2000) is outdated and fails to address risks for our children such as online pornography, sexting and staying safe online, as I discussed earlier in this chapter. The lack of relationships and sex education in schools has been described as a *'sexual health time bomb'* (Local Government Association 2017); storing up problems (for children) later in life, with many groups, including young people and parents calling for RSE to be made mandatory in all schools and for all schools to undertake a consistent approach to RSE. Findings from a recent survey of 16–24-year-olds by the Terence Higgins Trust (2016) found that 99 per cent of young people thought RSE should be mandatory in all schools; and of those surveyed, 1 in 7 had not received RSE. Critics of making RSE mandatory (such as Christian Concern and the Society for the Protection of Unborn Children) argue that it is not for the state to dictate what is taught in this area, rather it is up to parents to decide when to educate their children about sex and relationships.

However, years of campaigning from various groups such as the PSHE (Personal, Social and Health Education) Association, Barnados, End Violence Against Women Coalition, parents, teachers, headteachers and schools – who have all argued that it is vital for education to prepare young people for the challenges in life which have become even more pressing over the last ten years or so with the rise of social media and technology – have finally been successful.

In March 2017, the government announced that relationships and sex education is to be made compulsory in all secondary schools, including academies and free schools, in England; from September 2019. Relationships education in all primary schools will also become mandatory; however, sex education will continue to be non-statutory with the right to remove children from sex education lessons remaining with parents. The focus in primary schools will be on building healthy relationships and staying safe. Older children will develop their understanding of healthy adult relationships in more depth, sex education being delivered within that context.

The Rt. Hon Justine Greening, MP; Secretary of State for Education and Minister for Women and Equalities (2017) in a written statement said that:

> At the moment, many schools teach sex and relationships education, but it's not mandatory and; therefore, for many children, they are not coming out of our schools really being equipped to deal with the modern world or indeed be safe and protected from some of the very modern challenges that young people face on cyberbullying and sexting. What we're introducing is mandatory relationships and sex education in all secondary schools, but also mandatory relationships education in primary schools as well.

The Secretary of State for Education should be absolutely commended for her passion and commitment in bringing this much needed and wanted change to fruition; I hope that this will also lead the way for a revision of mandatory sex education for all upper KS2 pupils in light of research which also suggests that 10 and 11-year-olds are being increasingly exposed to sexting and pornography (ONS 2015); in addition, more research is much needed to determine the extent of this growing problem in primary schools.

The DFE will introduce a comprehensive programme of engagement which will set out suitable, age-appropriate (statutory) content for RSE. The government will not be prescriptive in how schools deliver RSE; instead, schools will have the freedom over how to deliver SRE so that their approach is inclusive and sensitive to the needs of their demographic and local community; for example, in the case of faith schools, they will be able to deliver RSE in accordance with the tenets of their faith.

Primary schools will, as is the case now, be required to publish a clear statement of their RSE policy – including what will be taught so that parents, who wish to withdraw their children from non-statutory sex education (not relationships education), can make an informed decision.

Teaching RSE in primary schools – what teachers need to know now!

Therefore, what do you, as a student teacher, need to know now about delivering RSE in primary schools at the moment? Before discussing what you need to know, take some time to reflect on the questions in the pause for thought.

Pause for thought

- At what age did you first have RSE at school?
- What were your experiences of RSE at school?
- What language was used? Could you access it?
- How did your experiences learning about sex make you feel?
- How about now? When discussing sex how does it make you feel?
- Does talking about sex make you behave differently? What about non-verbal cues? (You might or might not be aware about any non-verbal cues you are exhibiting).
- How do you feel about teaching RSE?
- What worries do you have and where will you go for support with this?

In England and Wales, the key points related to SRE (based on the 1996 Education Act) are as follows:

1 The sex education elements of the National Curriculum Science Order are mandatory for all pupils of primary school age. These cover anatomy, puberty, biological aspects of sexual reproduction and hormonal changes. When learning about puberty, children will learn:

- Biological names for parts of the body, including the sex organs (from Reception)
- Changes to sex organs and bodies during puberty, including physical and hormonal changes (upper KS2), including wet dreams and involuntary erections (KS2)
- About personal hygiene (lower and upper KS2)
- About menstruation and sanitary protection (upper KS2)

When learning about sexual reproduction, children will learn:

- That sexual intercourse is the way babies are conceived (KS2)
- Changes and human reproduction, the human life-cycle (including gestation) (KS2)
- How babies are born (KS2)
- Functions of reproductive organs (upper KS2) (DfE 2013)

2 *'Other elements of personal, social and health education (PSHE), including SRE, are non-statutory, but the DfE encourages all schools to develop their own SRE content with support from expert sources and incorporating PSHE.*

3 *All schools must provide, and make available for inspection, an up-to-date policy describing the content and organisation of SRE outside of national curriculum science. This is the school governors' responsibility in a state maintained school.*

4 *Primary schools should have a policy statement that describes the SRE provided or gives a statement of the decision not to provide SRE'* (FPA 2011)

In England and Wales, the Learning and Skills Act (2000) also noted in relation to SRE that:

1 *'Young people will learn about the nature of marriage and its importance for family life and bringing up children.*

2 *It is a school's and LEA's responsibility to ensure that young people are protected from teaching and materials which are inappropriate, having regard to the age and the religious and cultural background of the pupils concerned.*

3 *Parents have the right to withdraw their child from all or part of SRE provided outside national curriculum science'.*

In addition to this, the Department for Education and Employment (now the Department for Education) published guidance (in 2000) on the delivery of SRE through the PSHE framework. The guidance aims to help schools to plan SRE policy and practice and includes teaching strategies, working with parents, and confidentiality. The following is what you need to know as a student teacher:

1 When delivering SRE, there should be an emphasis on developing knowledge, skills and attitudes using appropriate teaching methods, teachers need CPD to be able to achieve this.

2 Primary schools should ensure that both boys and girls know about puberty before it begins.

3 Teachers should develop activities that will involve boys as well as girls.

4 Policies should be developed in consultation with parents, young people, teachers and governors.

5 SRE policy should be available for anyone to access on the school's website (Ofsted 2013).

6 All schools have a duty to ensure that the needs of children with special needs and learning disabilities are properly met.

7 The needs of all pupils should be met, regardless of sexual orientation or ethnicity.

8 SRE should be planned and delivered as part of PSHE and citizenship.

CASE STUDY 5.3 Children's questions?

- Why do people have sex?
- When should people have sex?
- What do I do if I swallow a condom?
- Where does a baby come from?
- Can women die having a baby?
- What does an abortion mean?
- What does being gay mean?
- Is it OK to be gay?
- What is sexual intercourse?
- What is the pill?
- What is an erection?
- I like someone in the class, what if he/she doesn't like me?

Pause for thought

- Which questions did you deem inappropriate or indeed appropriate?
- What parameters did you use to decide this?
- How do the questions make you feel?
- How would you deal with these questions in a classroom setting?

Therefore, when delivering SRE lessons, ensure that:

1 You are clear on the biology needed to understand Puberty and Reproduction in humans.

2 You understand the appropriate pedagogical approaches that are effective in delivering the RSE curriculum and appropriate to the age of the children you are teaching.

3 You have downloaded and read your placement school/s policy on RSE; then ensure that you discuss anything you are unsure of with your mentor, university tutor or person responsible for the policy in school.

4 You know what an **inappropriate question** is (again school policy) and how to deal with this; have a questions box that children can put their questions into (ensuring privacy and anonymity) – this also gives you the opportunity to vet any questions prior to discussing them with your class so that you are not drawn into providing more information than is appropriate for the age of the child and enable you to provide for the needs of children on an individual basis, for example, it is a teachers responsibility to acknowledge questions that are too explicit but which may need to be answered, at a parent's discretion, by a parent or carer; therefore, communication with parents and carers is of the utmost importance.

Remember it is important to find a way to deliver sex education factually, sensitively and without embarrassment; you should never be drawn into answering questions about your own sex life or indeed anyone else's.

5 You know the curriculum content and *what you are not teaching, this might very well vary depending on the type of school you are in*; for example, a child might ask you about abortion, contraception or homosexuality – how will you address this? It is perfectly acceptable to tell a child that a particular subject cannot be discussed in school or indeed refer them to their parents (remember parents will be informed that children are having RSE lessons in school; outlines of what is being taught will be available to parents on the school website; parents will therefore be informed that their children might very well ask questions of them regarding RSE at home). I would then advise you to inform your school mentor and university tutor about what has been raised and how you addressed this – clear communication is important.

6 *You should not be* delivering RSE without training – consider your needs as a learner student teacher and discuss this with your mentor and university tutor.

7 You understand Safeguarding – ensure you have read your school's policy on Safeguarding in relation to delivering RSE (this might be included in the SRE policy or separately in the Safeguarding policy); there might be, for example, a disclosure by a child of abuse, or you might have concerns about what a child is saying in relation to RSE, in this instance you would be expected to follow the school's Safeguarding and/or Child Protection Policy.

8 Most importantly, if in doubt or if you are unsure about anything to do with delivering lessons about RSE, seek support and advice from your school mentor, university tutor, school Science/PSHE co-ordinator and Science/PSHE lead at university.

All children are entitled to high-quality RSE, to keep them safe from harm and develop positive and healthy attitudes to sex and relationships. Student teachers and teachers can only deliver this if they have received the best and most effective CPD relating to delivering RSE.

Summary

- Children are naturally curious and their curiosity should be fostered.
- Science can provoke children to ask questions which are controversial which teachers might find challenging to address; however, using a wide range of pedagogical approaches as discussed in this chapter (and other chapters in this book); teachers ensuring that their subject and pedagogical knowledge

for science is strong; schools having clear and informative policies for the provision of science which are shared with parents and pupils alike; and schools ensuring that they have positive avenues of communication with parents based on mutual respect, will enable any primary teacher of science to feel confident to address their *pupils' curiosity without crushing it!*

- Evolution is a scientific theory, heavily substantiated by a plethora of scientific evidence and should be taught as such – not as a belief.

- Evolution lessons in primary schools are not an opportunity to have a theological debate about the existence of God!

- Student teachers must be clear on the scientific misconceptions related to evolution and ensure they know how to identify and thus address these.

- The biology curriculum for sex education is statutory; parents cannot withdraw their children from learning this.

- From 2019, the new curriculum for relationships and sex education will be implemented in both primary and secondary schools, this will include academies and free schools; relationships education in primary schools will become mandatory.

- Parents are less likely to withdraw their children from the non-statutory aspects of sex and relationships education if they are clear about what content will be delivered and in what guise – schools need to ensure that they build strong, honest relationships with parents for this to happen and use appropriate materials when discussing sex and relationships with children.

- As a student teacher (or teacher) ensure that you have read all the school policies and guidance on delivering RSE – if in doubt, seek advice from more experienced colleagues. This is especially important if you feel a Safeguarding issue has been raised, never ignore this or any signs that ring alarm bells; no-one will think you are being silly or that you are wasting their time. *Ultimately you are accountable for, and have a duty of care to, the pupils you teach (Teachers' Standards 7 and Part 2).*

Recommended reading

Allen, M. (2014). *Misconceptions in Primary Science*. Open University Press.
Cooper, V. and Martinez, A. (2012). *Laying the Foundations: A Practical Guide to Sex and Relationships Education in Primary Schools, (2nd Edition)*. National Children's Bureau.
Emmerson, L. and Lees, J. (2013). *Let's Get It Right: A Toolkit for Involving Primary School Children in Reviewing Sex and Relationships Education*. National Children's Bureau.
Horlock, J., Naylor, S. and Moyles, J. (2015). *Let's Talk about Evolution*. Millgate House.
Wooley, R. (2010). *Tackling Controversial Issues in the Primary School*. Routledge.
http://www.sexeducationforum.org.uk/media/17706/sreadvice.pdf
http://www.pshe-association.org.uk/curriculum-and-resources/resources/sex-and-relationship-education-sre-21st-century.

Chapter 6
Children's Ideas – Promoting Curiosity

The important thing is to not stop questioning. Curiosity has its own reason for existence. One cannot help but be in awe when one contemplates the mysteries of eternity, of life, of the marvellous structures of reality. It is enough if one tries merely to comprehend a little of this mystery each day.

Albert Einstein

Chapter objectives

By the end of this chapter you will have an understanding of:

- What we mean by curiosity in science
- Why it is important for children to maintain their natural curiosity
- How we can promote curiosity in science
- Ways in which we can use children's curiosity to move towards a more scientific understanding of the world.

Introduction

If science is about finding out the answers to questions, how do we encourage children to ask the questions in the first place? This chapter looks at how we can tap into the ideas that children have already about their world, help them to ask questions that can be investigated in scientific ways, and offer them the appropriate experiences to refine their ideas towards more scientific explanations. The chapter explores issues to do with children's innate curiosity, and how teachers can harness that curiosity while still fulfilling the obligations of the national curriculum for England and Wales. We consider why it seems that as children move through the primary setting, they sometimes seem to lose that curiosity and excitement about the world, and what we as practitioners can do to ameliorate that decline and maintain the intrinsic satisfaction of asking 'why' and 'how'. In this chapter, we also reflect on why it is so important to us all that the children continue to develop their ideas and curiosity, and to explore why taking a 'playful' approach to learning should lead the way.

We hope that this chapter will challenge some of you to take risks with your practice that will enable the children to lead the way, and that will enable you to create exciting and engaging opportunities that will foster curiosity, not just at primary school, but throughout their lives. We hope to encourage you, too, to be curious and to take a questioning attitude towards the world around you so that you can serve as a model to the children.

What is curiosity in primary science?

Well, quite simply it is asking questions! It is children wanting to know about things that they notice. It is children seeking explanations for their world, and the things that interest them. Nietzsche (1844–1900) said that a 'thinker sees his own actions as experiments and questions, as attempts to find something out'. That seems to fit well with the Piagetian concept of children constructing their understanding of the world through their experiences, and our own experiences of young children tell us that it is their curiosity about the world that is the key motivator of all that they do. Children who are happy and in a secure class environment, where questions are valued and encouraged; where questions are seen as learning opportunities need not lose their innate curiosity as they move through the school.

Encouraging children to ask questions has its difficulties however, as children can easily get self-conscious about questions if they are not respected by the teacher or other children, and the modelling of questions based on curiosity and wondering is a crucial aspect of the pedagogical content knowledge (Shulman 1986) that the teacher needs to draw on.

CASE STUDY 6.1

Year 2 children were studying life cycles and exploring how humans change as they grow. The mother of one of the children in the class, who was expecting another baby, had been invited in to answer the children's questions. One of the working scientifically requirements for year 2 (National Curriculum 2013) is for children to raise and answer questions that help them become familiar with the life processes, and to understand how humans grow from babies to adults. The class teacher, seizing the opportunity of cross-curricular links, was using the literacy lesson the day before the visit to teach the children about question marks, and so had planned for the children to write the questions they thought they would like to ask the impending visitor.

One child wrote: 'do you like chocolate?' as a question to ask.

What are your initial thoughts on this?

How is this question linked to the science topic?

Does this scenario meet the working scientifically requirements?

Does this promote curiosity?

It is evident that several things were happening here. The first is that the teacher was using the science to promote the literacy, and in doing so lost the impact and the link to the science; it was the literacy driving the lesson, not the science. Thus, the children were being asked to think of questions out of context, and without the visitor being in the classroom, did not have the excitement or motivation to be curious enough to ask questions about the growing baby. The second is that the plan for the science when the children had the visit from the expectant mother was lifted directly from a published scheme, and the teacher, by not planning for the children in her class had lost the enthusiasm and passion that would model the curiosity for the children. Thirdly, although a lovely way of reinforcing the home/school links by having a parent coming to talk to the children, it was unable to capture the natural and spontaneous curiosity 'in the moment'. It would be interesting to know if that child asked the visitor whether she liked chocolate …

> The best science teachers, seen as part of this survey, set out to 'first maintain curiosity' in their pupils. (Maintaining Curiosity, Ofsted 2013: 4)

Thus, in the science lessons we prepare for the children in our class, we should ensure that we contextualize the learning and as much as possible try to allow children to explore using things that are relevant and interesting to them, so that they begin to move towards scientific explanations. Exploration should definitely not be confined to the Early Years and Foundation Stage! Of course, not all of the questions children will ask lend themselves to being answered through an investigative type of enquiry. Some will need a research enquiry to find the answers because they are not suitable to 'test' out in the primary classroom. For example, a question such as 'why do leaves fall off trees in autumn?' cannot be answered through a test that is viable in the primary classroom, but as we have seen in Chapter 4, research is a perfectly acceptable part of scientific enquiry.

> Through building up a body of key foundational knowledge and concepts, pupils should be encouraged to recognise the power of rational explanation and develop a sense of excitement and curiosity about natural phenomena. (National Curriculum 2013: 3)

Pause for thought

- Can you help to maintain children's curiosity by linking questions to your topic?

For example, if KS2 history curriculum (2013) were studying the impact of the first railways, it could begin by a trip to a transport museum. Gentle guiding and modelling of curiosity, and 'I wonder how …?' questions posed by the teacher could link the study to science by considering the impact of food being brought from the countryside to the cities to feed the rapid growth in urban living. I wonder how food was kept fresh for the journeys? Can we research that and compare to preservative methods used nowadays by investigating the effect of salt, sugar, dried, tinned and freezing as means of stopping bacteria developing? Thus develops the excitement of the yucky growing mould on various foods in different environments. Children could put bread in the staff room freezer, in a plastic bag, on the windowsill above the radiator, in a cupboard for example. And so the questions can keep coming as children become more curious, and with guidance from the teacher lead on to learning about Marie Curie and Lister and their discoveries, and further the relevance of vaccinations in real life. The opportunities are great for the creative practitioner to help children be both curious and to understand what science is for.

Remember to consult your copy of 'Be Safe, 2014' to understand how to handle moulds in the classroom!

Why should children be curious?

Well, they just *are* curious – if we let them be! We need children to be curious so that they want to find out the answers to their questions and seek explanations for what they see around them. In doing so, they increase their understanding and knowledge. Their curiosity gives us the opportunity to develop their enquiry skills: the skills to evaluate and analyse, the respect for evidence, and to develop children's scientific literacy. According to Harlen et al. (2010), the main reason for science education is to enable everyone to be able to take informed decisions and actions that will promote their own well-being and that of society. As we write this, there are leaders of developed nations promoting actions based on discredited science, which could affect the health of many children if they are not protected from measles; if contracted in vulnerable children measles can be fatal. A curious individual, it is hoped, would investigate such rhetoric and make decisions based on their science understanding. Harlen (ibid.) goes on to say that the science we do with our pupils throughout their schooling should aim to develop curiosity and enjoyment of doing science activity as well as understanding. It is through these endeavours that children's scientific literacy, as well as their enquiry skills is developed. Furthermore, Teacher's standard 4 states that teachers should promote love of learning and intellectual curiosity (DfE 2012).

How can teachers promote children's curiosity?

Are you curious? Do you model that 'I wonder why …' attitude? Or when you take the children outside for their learning (you do that, don't you?) allow your fear of spiders to show? Positive attitudes and a sense of curiosity come from the teacher, and from the teacher's passion and enthusiasm. We sometimes wonder how many teachers are explicit in letting the children in their class know what science is for. Do the children in your class know that science is a way of explaining the world around them, and that is why they do it? Do the children you teach know what science is *for*? If children can be helped to see science as relevant to their own questions about the world, then they are likely to be more engaged and motivated, and want to find the answers to their questions.

Consider some of these ways of promoting curiosity in children

1. 'Hooking the children' in to the learning at the beginning of the topic.

Don't be afraid of giving children facts. It might seem that throughout this book we have been advocating children engaging in enquiry-led and child-led learning. We are both passionate about that, it is true, and this is supported by findings from the Royal Society (2010: 89) who are adamant that science needs to be enquiry based at all levels, and that a fact-based approach 'conflicts with children's natural curiosity and exploratory instincts'. However, that doesn't mean we can't use our more developed knowledge and understanding to intrigue children, and to 'hook them in', so that they are excited to find out for themselves. This becomes a form of scaffolding whereby you have given the children something to think about and extend their knowledge.

Pause for thought

- Did you know that woodlice, those little crustaceans that you find under stones and leaves in the garden, make the most excellent mothers?
- If you were about to embark on the topic of investigating local habitats for year 2, how might this intriguing fact encourage curiosity?
- How could children find out about this?
- What kind of enquiry might they want to do to find out if this is true?

Similarly, by creating a 'Wow' moment for the children (Feasey 2005), we can engage and excite children's interest, which leads to questions. Oliver (2006: 28) suggests that 'science cannot be taught well or received well without feeling some magic in everyday occurrences in nature'. We teachers can create some of that magic in the classroom by bringing in unexpected things to the classroom. One thing we do for our very first science session with our PGCE students is to bring in a handful of things we have found in our local neighbourhood, which stimulates intrigue. As these sessions are always in September, there is a wealth of natural objects that can be discovered even in an urban environment. We usually bring in a bruised apple that has fallen to the pavement from an overhanging apple tree; a plane tree seed ball, which is rarely identified by the students; a beautiful conker with its spiky casing; a handful of hazel nuts from a tree planted by a forgetful squirrel one year in a neighbour's garden; and last year, a handful of deformed acorns which after research through the Royal Horticultural Society website, discovered that the deformation was caused by a wasp which laid eggs in many of the early developing acorns (you see, we're still passionately curious). As we pass these few everyday, everywhere things around the groups, it is wonderful to see them beginning to ask questions of each other, as it demonstrates the wonder of the natural world. In case you're thinking that you couldn't do something like this, let me reassure you that we live in urban South London, and collect these things before the start of term when walking or in the park.

Another way of intriguing the children is to demonstrate some counter-intuitive science after asking the children what they think would happen. Look at the example in case study 6.2, and have a think about it. There are plenty of ideas about counter-intuitive science, either through some of the recommended readings, or science websites that have been listed at the end of chapters.

CASE STUDY 6.2

An example of a demonstration of counter-intuitive science is to have three balloons blown up to different sizes, and 'float' them in a stream of warm air from a ceiling-pointed hairdryer. If you ask most children (and indeed adults) to predict the order in which they would float, starting with the one that would be nearest to the nozzle of the hairdryer, the answer given would be largest at the bottom and smallest at the top.

Try it, and see what happens!

Can you use your science understanding to explain the outcome?

You could also try what McCrory (2011) calls the 'gross factor'. When teaching about micro-organisms, allow an orange to go mouldy (put it in a plastic bag before you show the children for health and safety reasons), and then introduce your new class 'pets'. The children will always be intrigued by how disgusting it is, and it leads neatly to investigating, and observing over time, the conditions for growth and reproduction of micro-organisms.

An important aspect of creating 'wow' moments or intriguing hooks for the children is that they should be followed by giving the children time to explore, to 'play' with the artefacts, equipment or resources to develop their questions and hypotheses before identifying emerging themes and planning how to develop these into enquiry questions (Hardman and Luke 2016). The next sections address these ideas.

2. Encouraging questions that allows for child-led enquiry learning.

The question that arose in case study 6.1 shows how easy it is for questions to not be relevant to the learning you want to guide your children to attain. So, if you want them to ask questions, how can you begin to encourage and develop more 'scientific' questions? That is, questions that can be turned into an enquiry, where children not only find some answers and ways of explaining, but are learning how to 'do' science at the same time. One way is to develop a 'wonder wall' where children know they are going to be learning about a particular science topic, and are encouraged to write any questions they have about the topic on to a post-it note which is displayed in the classroom. This is a bit of a leap of faith for the teacher, and emphasizes the need for secure subject knowledge, because this must happen before you plan the particular lessons. From these questions you can encourage children to collaboratively decide which ones can be answered through scientific enquiry, and roll out the lessons based on the questions that the children have decided can be answered this way. Even though not all the questions lend themselves to being investigated, by the end of your series of lessons on the topic, most questions will be able to be answered with the new knowledge and understanding that the children have acquired. The vital thing with the wonder walls is that they should be revisited every science lesson, and which question is being investigated should be made explicit. Any that still can't be answered at the end of the unit of work should be able to be researched through the internet or subject books, which, remember, is a valid form of scientific enquiry in its own right, and this demonstrates that all questions are valued.

Figure 6.1 An example of a year 5 wonder wall, based on 'The Big Question' (Holligan 2013) where children's questions have been valued and displayed

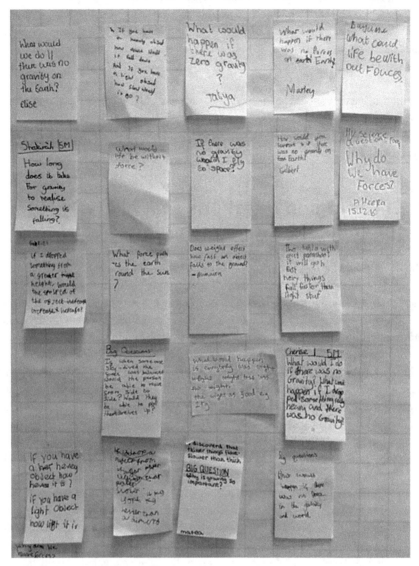

3. Allowing children to 'play' before starting the topic.

Play is our brain's favourite way of learning. (Diane Ackerman)

Play is a curious word in primary education. In the EYFS, we expect to see children playing, and practitioners know that through engagement with the real-world materials and resources, along with rich questioning from adults and peers, children begin to form their ideas about the world. Some children play alone and can demonstrate deep concentration as they engage with the resources. In all of this exploring the world, they are said to be 'playing'. They are, in fact, doing important and serious learning. They are investigating and either constructing or co-constructing their emerging understanding of how the world works. Asoko (2002) contends that it doesn't always follow that practical science and experience always leads to accepted scientific facts, but it is not crucial if their ideas are still emergent at this stage because in the nature of the spiral curriculum (Bruner 1960) they will revisit their ideas again and again, deepening their understanding and moving towards more scientifically accepted explanations as they do so.

It begs the question then: why don't children have the opportunity to continue to do this important and serious learning, this 'play', as they move through the primary years? In fact, we would contend that older children, even in Key Stage Two, should be given the opportunity to play. Does it sound better if we use the word 'explore' instead? Apart from the well-recognized cognitive benefits of interaction with concrete materials (Russell and McGuigan 2016), exploring is good fun, engaging and motivating children to have ownership of their learning. We often ask our PGCE students: where does it say that children aren't learning if they are having fun?

A further idea that you could employ in your science teaching if you are a Key Stage One or Two practitioner is to plan opportunities for children to engage in role-play to deepen their understanding of the science they are learning. For example, in communicating their findings, children could present their learning in the role of a news presenter, or chat show host asking others in their group to explain what they have learnt. This takes away some of the difficulties some children have of always having to write about their science, as has been discussed in the chapter on assessment. Some of the strategies used in literacy lessons can be used to great effect in science. A 'conscience alley' can be used at the end of a topic that has environmental implications or health choices, whereby children draw on all their knowledge of the topic to convince themselves of the benefits of particular courses of action. This strategy also requires children to collaborate, take a perspective that they might not agree with (which develops the beginnings of criticality), and is inclusive of all children, as all can put forward a point of view.

If children take particular roles (such as recorder, equipment manager, time keeper, presenter) in their enquiries, this also allows them to value the importance of responsibility to the group. The role-playing of abstract concepts, for example, as the bonds of solids, liquids and gases; or electrical circuits, allows children to visualize some of the scientific ideas that they can't experience for themselves at the primary level, and thus deepens and enhances understanding of tricky concepts. This again is inclusive practice as these strategies allow children to engage in the science at their own level.

> ### CASE STUDY 6.3
>
> We have seen far less evidence of 'play' in the older year groups with the exception of enquiry-led science lessons. In a year 3 lesson on magnets, children were instructed to play with the magnets and make notes on how they interacted with each other and with objects in the classroom. Although children were not given a choice in the activity, so the learning was not completely self-directed, they were still able to use resources set out by the teacher to independently problem solve. Children with different levels of prior knowledge explored the magnets in different ways. One child already seemed to know much about the laws of magnetism and quickly began devising an experiment with a ruler to measure how close the magnets had to be to each other to attract or repel each other. Many other children didn't know about the different poles so spent their time observing which poles would attract and which would repel. Everybody, using varying methods, built upon their own prior knowledge and experience to deepen their learning about magnetism and developed a curiosity that, as would be expected, encouraged further enquiry.
>
> Would you consider this to be personalized learning?
>
> As a reflective practitioner, building on your assessment for learning, what opportunities would you plan for the children after this lesson?

It is our belief, and indeed, our experience, that children learn more and ask more questions (the very bedrock of science enquiry) when they are relaxed and having fun. That is, when they are 'playing'.

4. Developing children's autonomy and ownership of the science enquiry.

Piaget claimed that for a child to have intrinsic desire to drive their learning forward, then they have to be curious but also in control of their own learning (Aubrey and Riley 2016). Peacock (2008) talks about allowing children to use drawing to demonstrate their ideas, which triggers many questions from the children. He continues that children need to see that their questions are taken seriously, as we have been saying and that they will have the opportunity to investigate them. This develops a sense of ownership of the learning in the children, that their questions about the world are valid and serious, which in turn develops their autonomy. If children's enquiry skills have been systematically developed throughout their time in primary school, and they have been allowed to plan their own investigations, rather than the teacher micro-manage them (as has been argued in chapter 4), then children are well on their way to becoming independent learners. Teachers, of course, have to be able to stand back and suspend judgement, possibly many times along the way, and to foster in the children a belief that mistakes are an important part of learning. Without making mistakes, in deciding how to carry out their own investigations, they cannot learn to be decision makers and develop this autonomy. If children's investigations uphold their predictions, then that is great, because it convinces them of what they already knew. For an investigation to not work out the way they expected teaches them something new, so their knowledge and understanding of doing science is extended, and they make progress.

The notion of encouraging and developing children's sense of autonomy with regard to their learning appears to us to be an important one. Since children are likely to be more engaged in the learning when they can take ownership of it, to foster autonomy must also, surely, foster metacognition. Where children are aware of their own learning, with 'minds-on', rather than mechanistically doing what the teacher told them to do, then a 'growth mindset' develops in the children (Dweck 2017). This is what creates our 'thinkers', surely? Who knows, perhaps you have the next Einstein in your class.

> achievement was highest where pupils were involved in planning, carrying out and evaluating investigations that, in some part, they had suggested themselves. They learnt best when they could see how the science they were studying linked to real world experiences, revealed more about the 'big ideas' in science, ... Learning in this fashion engages and enthuses pupils, develops their natural curiosity, and motivates them to find out more. (Ofsted 2013: 10)

How can children's curiosity be used to move children to more scientific ideas?

As you can see from the case study in the previous section, allowing children to explore can not only be very effective assessment for learning, it leads us as practitioners, to be able to plan for effective provision to build on the children's initial and emerging ideas about both scientific concepts, along with opportunities to develop skills of working scientifically. Children's own curiosity, harnessed through their questions, enables us as practitioners to plan the next steps, to challenge children's current thinking at an appropriate level and create some cognitive conflict. According to Piaget's (1961) model of cognitive development, it is this that leads to transformative learning. This is done through children engaging in scientific enquiry; when they have ownership of the outcomes and thus, present themselves with the evidence that changes understanding. Crucially the role of the practitioner is to capture the moment when children experience this cognitive conflict, so that through dialogic teaching (Alexander, 2004), we can scaffold the children's understandings until they have reached a stage of cognitive equilibrium (Piaget 1961). This involves knowing the children you are teaching and their individual needs, so that you can practise effective assessment for learning 'in the moment' as your children are engaging in their scientific enquiry. From this knowledge about where the children are in their understanding, you will be in a strong position to plan exciting engaging lessons that will consolidate the children's scientific understanding, and they will achieve well and make good progress.

CASE STUDY 6.4

The schools visited that made science interesting for their pupils, both primary and secondary schools, raised achievement in science. In both phases, the most effective approach seen was through practically based investigations. Pupils experienced the scientific phenomena for themselves and then used that experience to raise their own further questions, thereby maintaining curiosity. In the best practice in all schools, pupils could answer the question, 'what is it for?' when asked by teachers and inspectors. At lesson level, pupils contributed to the questions that were going to be investigated. For example, a Year 5 teacher asked pupils, 'What would you like to find out about sound?' The response included some very challenging questions such as 'What does a sound wave look like?' and 'How do you know a bat can hear higher [frequencies] than a dog?' (Ofsted 2013: 40)

Pause for thought

- What does the science lead in your setting have to say about children's curiosity?
- How is the curiosity shown by the children you teach captured and utilized to give ownership and autonomy to the children?
- Are the children in Key Stage One and Key Stage Two still allowed to 'play' in science, and are opportunities planned for activities such as role-play to consolidate understanding?
- How could you make a difference in the promotion of curiosity as a prerequisite for effective science learning in your class?

The idea of children engaging in child-led enquiry, where they are exploiting their own curiosity and autonomy in order to make progress in scientific understanding is one that needs a rigorous overview of the whole-school approach to the science provision. The provision of long-term planning and monitoring of the received curriculum, and how we are assessing the children's progress are concepts explored in Chapters 4 and 7.

Millions saw the apple fall; Newton was the only one who asked, why? (Bernard Baruch)

Summary

- The importance of children developing their own questions to investigate
- The importance of teacher's promoting children's curiosity
- The role of play and exploration in developing children's knowledge and understanding of science concepts and ways of working
- The value of children's autonomy in planning and doing their own investigations
- The teacher's role in moving children from being curious to more scientific explanations

Recommended reading

Bostrum, C. (2016). *Experiencing Child-led Science in Science Week*. Primary Science No 142. Available at www.ase.org.uk

Roden, J. (2015). *An Introduction to Science* (Chapter 3, pp. 47–74) in Driscoll, P., Lambrith, A. and Roden, J. (2015) *The Primary Curriculum: A Creative Approach*. Sage.

Hardman, S. and Luke, S. (2016). *How can you Make the Most of those 'Wow Moments'?* Primary Science No 141. Available at www.ase.org.uk

Myers, D., McGrory, M. and Westgate, C. (2016). *Curiouser and Curiouser: Supporting Children's Independent Enquiry Skills*. Primary Science No 142. Available at www.ase.org.uk

Phethean, K. (2008). *When are you too old to 'Play' in Science*. Primary Science No 105. Available at www.ase.org.uk

Rivett, A. C., Harrison, T. G. and Shallcross, D. E. (2009). *The Art of Chemistry*. Primary Science No 110. Available at www.ase.org.uk

Chapter 7
Assessing Children in Science

Tell me and I forget. Teach me and I remember. Involve me and I learn.

Benjamin Franklin

Chapter objectives

By the end of this chapter you will have developed an understanding of:

- What effective assessment is when assessing science;
- What AfL and formative assessment are in relation to science;
- The challenges of assessing working scientifically and how they can be overcome;
- Effective next-step marking;
- Reporting assessment to parents.

Introduction

Assessment in science is not easy or indeed straightforward – learning itself is not simple or linear; the inclusion of working scientifically to deliver the primary science curriculum has, for some schools and teachers, been problematic. This chapter discusses those challenges and the recent changes to assessment in primary schools, including the sampling of assessment in science taking place in year 6 throughout schools across England and Wales which started in 2014 and will be completed in 2018. In addition to this, the debate between formative assessment and assessment for learning (AfL) in relation to assessing science effectively is discussed; ideas and solutions are offered in relation to assessing scientific enquiry focusing on how teachers can build a robust picture of their pupils' scientific knowledge, understanding and enquiry skills by assessing in a multitude of ways. There has been a culture shift in recent years in primary schools in England and Wales to next-step mark children's work as a process of assessment; we discuss the positives and possible pit-falls of this, providing examples of how this can be achieved effectively while reflecting on the role of feedback. We examine the roles and responsibilities that teachers have when assessing children's progress and attainment (Teachers' Standards 2 and 6) including a focus on reporting to parents – an area of assessment not often included in books about primary science.

Assessment in science – the ultimate challenge for the novice teacher

In our experience, assessment of scientific knowledge and understanding as well as process skills can be challenging for an experienced teacher and often daunting for a student teacher. Findings from the CFE (2017) state that around 75 per cent of primary teachers feel confident in assessing science which is positive; however, what can be the reason for a lack of confidence when assessing primary science? Often, assessment in science causes anxiety for our students because of a number of reasons:

a) Poor modelling of assessment of science in some placement schools;

b) The use of assessment scaffolds or criteria which are ambiguous and sometimes meaningless;

c) A lack of understanding by some schools of what assessment in science entails, for example the obsession some schools have with ensuring everything is recorded in books;

d) Subject knowledge of the novice teacher can make assessment in science challenging;

e) Students not understanding the steps to success (or success criteria needed) for the children to achieve the learning objective (LO);

f) AfL can be challenging; it has many generic features but there are some aspects of AfL that can be honed to assess science learning;

g) The classroom climate is key; behaviour for learning must be established (not behaviour management) and novice teachers can struggle with this during their PGCE placements and NQT year. *'It is crucial that a co-constructivist, non-threatening environment is established in order for pupils to feel able to express their ideas and allow the teacher to establish what the pupils know, what they don't know and what they partly know – their scientific misconceptions – and to develop teaching that will move their understanding on'* (Hodgson and Pyle 2010: 1);

h) Concerns over the question of how much evidence and what type of evidence is needed to show that pupils are making progress in their scientific knowledge and understanding as well as their process skills.

Recent changes to assessment in primary schools

Assessment procedures have changed in primary schools from using APP (Assessing Pupils Progress based on the NC Level descriptors) to schools having more autonomy in how they record and monitor assessment; however, what all schools will have in common is that they must assess the statutory requirements of the primary national curriculum (2013) and must report on below, expected or exceeding age-related expectations (ARE). In two thirds of primary schools inspected by Ofsted (2011, 2013), assessment in science was found to be 'Good to Outstanding' (Oftsed 2011, 2013); therefore, changes to assessment procedures need to become embedded in schools.

Pause for thought

- What is assessment?
- What is formative/summative assessment?
- What is AfL?
- When do you, as a teacher, assess, or how often does your school placement teacher assess science?
- What and how are you recording assessment in a science lesson?
- What concerns do you have about assessment in science?

What is assessment in primary science?

Black and Harrison (2004) argue that there are four key principles in the assessment of science which include the following:

1 *Teachers must start from where the learners are* (eliciting prior knowledge is key to this), *as learners need to be active agents in reconstructing their ideas;*

2 *Learning has to be done by the learners and not done for them!* One of the best pieces of advice I was given by an excellent head-teacher that I worked for is that the children need to work 80 per cent of the time, teachers work 20 per cent of the time. She did not mean that teachers only teach 20 per cent of the time and then put their feet up for the rest of the lesson. Far from it, what she meant was that the teacher needed to be the facilitator of a child's learning, enabling children to learn and make progress; ensuring that children are actively engaged while using AfL techniques to enable progress within a lesson;

3 *In order to learn, the learners must understand the learning target–* this is a key point, ideally children should be involved in creating their targets to achieve with the class teacher;

4 *Learners need to talk about their learning and reflect on it*!

It is important for the student teacher to know that functions of assessment are:

1 To inform planning for future teaching;

2 To inform children about their own learning and progress and involve them in the process of assessment;

3 To inform subsequent teachers and the school about children's learning, progress and attainment;

4 To inform parents about their children's learning and progress (Sewell 2014).

Types of assessment in the primary science classroom

There are a number of ways to assess children's progress and attainment in primary science which are:

1 Criterion-referenced assessment – this type of assessment is based on each learner's performance against a set of criteria regardless of the performance of others; ARE in the primary national curriculum are an example of this.

2 Norm-referencing – this type of assessment is where the expectation of the average learner is known and used; ultimately this type of assessment tests the test taker against his or her peers – in science, this would include end of unit or year tests, SATS tests and as children get older, GCSEs and A Levels.

3 Diagnostic assessment – this type of assessment is used to identify areas of strengths and weaknesses, typically to address gaps in knowledge and understanding.

4 Ipsative assessment – which we argue is one of the most important forms of assessment in teaching and learning in science. This type of assessment measures what one learner can do with reference solely to their past performance. It focuses on the progress of the individual learner and for this to be effective, the learner must be involved – being aware of past performance and how to better this is an integral aspect of children progressing throughout their school careers (Ward and Remnant, 2016).

Pause for thought

Think about a time where you have made progress and achieved –

1 How were you enabled to do this by others?

2 How did you enable yourself to achieve?

3 How did you know how to succeed?

4 What did success look like to you?

Formative assessment and/or assessment for learning?

Pause for thought

- What form might formative assessment/AfL take in general and when assessing science?

There has been some confusion about what formative assessment is, as there have been many definitions for this; for example, assessment is learning or balanced assessment. In the UK, 'Formative assessment and AoL are terms which usually describe the same thing' (Clarke 2014:3). They both play an important role in the primary science classroom to enabling learners to learn and make progress via better teaching (Wiliam 2012). AoL has been defined as: *'The process of seeking and interpreting evidence for use by learners and their teachers to decide where learners are in their learning, where they need to go and how best to get there'* (Assessment Reform Group 2002: 2).

What does this include when assessing science learning?

- A learning culture – where there is a belief that everyone can succeed, as we noted at the beginning of the chapter, behaviour for learning is key not simply behaviour management. Being quiet does not necessarily mean children are actively engaged in their learning. This is embedded in Dweck's (2006, 2017) notion of a Growth Mindset as discussed in Chapter 1 where children use their metacognitive skills to be successful

- Children should be involved at the planning stage to ensure their ownership over and engagement in learning

- As discussed in Chapters 1, 3 and 4, social constructivism is key for children to learn from each other (More Knowledgeable Other), and access differentiated activities including challenge for all (Chapter 8)

- Clear LOs which must be shared with the children (Clarke 2014) so that they understand the expectations of the lesson; resist doing this at the start of the lesson in science so that you can elicit the children's curiosity first as discussed in Chapter 4

- Success criteria and steps to success must be just that; they can also be co-constructed with the children (promoting active learning, engagement and understanding by the children of how to succeed). They can then be used for the children to use when self-assessing – this does not necessarily need to happen at the end of the lesson, it is good practice for children to monitor this as they go along

- Discovering children's alternative ideas and scientific misconceptions is a very valuable benefit of AfL because by establishing if there are any misconceptions (for example, believing that light travels straight into your eyes) you can then plan a way to challenge and reconstruct this. Developing a classroom climate in which pupils are willing to discuss their ideas and are not afraid of being wrong is crucial to finding out and addressing pupil misconceptions (Allen 2014)

- Effective questioning – use Bloom's Revised Taxonomy (2001) or SOLO Taxonomy (Biggs and Collis 1982) to enhance your questioning skills to have a direct impact on your children's thinking skills; ask open and effective questions which form part of 'in the moment' feedback. In science, questioning can be used to *'Encourage comparison; classify, group and recognize exceptions; enable children to predict and hypothesize– and should encourage teachers to delve deeper into their children's conceptual learning'*(Black and Harrison 2004)

- Children also need to be giving opportunities to ask questions to scaffold their own thinking and understanding, reveal their ideas and possible misconceptions as well as investigate and find things out for themselves which is satisfying and highly motivational (Harlen and Qualter 2014)

- Chin (2004) also identifies that *'Questioning is key to active and meaningful learning and is the cornerstone of scientific enquiry'* (2004: 107) which by now, you know, is an incredibly important part of the primary science curriculum

- Ensure you monitor the children's learning throughout the lesson via dialogue and talk (Hargreaves, 2007) which can be an AfL technique which is underestimated and sometimes discouraged because of student teachers' fears that children are not on task and might be talking about something else, again this comes back to teachers ensuring that they have high expectations of behaviour for learning – a science classroom should never be silent

- Modelling is important, not only by you as the teacher but also use examples of what the children have produced to share

- Feedback needs to focus on success and where improvements are required. Effective feedback should initiate thinking, enabling the learner 'to discuss his or her thoughts with the teacher or a peer' in order to instigate improvement; it should prompt immediate action; it should relate back to the steps to success or success criteria and it should allow learners to match their own judgement of quality against that of the teacher or peer. It may also direct learners where they can go for help, for example Shirley Clarke's the 5 Bs, (2014) or indeed what they need to do to improve their work – next-step marking for example (Black and Harrison 2004; Nottingham and Nottingham 2017)

- Peer feedback is an effective way to ensure that children can improve their work immediately during the lesson

- Mini-plenaries; do not only need to be used at the end of the lesson; they can be used effectively at points during the lesson where expectations need reinforcing or the teacher needs to model. When used at the end of the lesson, they should be used to summarize learning against the success criteria (Black and Wiliam 2009; Hodgson and Pyle 2010; Clarke 2014).

Science provides the means by which learners can interact with the world around them and develop ideas about the phenomena they experience. So, when they attempt activities such as germinating seeds, their studies in science equip them with ways to observe and question what is happening. Through experiments they can begin to work out and predict what might happen if conditions for the growing plant change. To be able to learn science in this way, students need help in developing process skills to investigate and communication skills to question and discuss findings. Formative assessment fits well into this learning scenario, since its purpose is for teachers to sift the rich data that arise in classroom discussion and activity, so that professional judgements can be made about the next steps in learning (Black and Harrison 2004:3).

Figure 7.1 A year 2 study of plants – with thanks to Aveley Primary school, Essex

Next-step marking – enabling learning and progress via effective feedback where appropriate

Pause for thought

- How would you define effective feedback?
- Think of a time you have received what you perceive to be effective feedback, what did this look like?
- In order to receive feedback, what attributes does the learner need to have?

What is the point of feedback?

Feedback should enable children to close the gap between what they know and where they are to where they want or need to be next. As Nottingham and Nottingham (2017: 10) argue, feedback should help learners answer the following three questions:

1 'What am I trying to achieve?
2 How much progress have I made so far?
3 What should I do next?'

Effective feedback is central to children making progress in their learning (Hattie 2012; Black and Wiliam 1998). First of all, it is important to understand that:

1 All feedback is not necessarily effective feedback that has an impact on learning;

2 Feedback does not always have to be written down to 'prove' that feedback has been given;

3 Feedback can happen at any time during the lesson or day and not simply reserved for the plenary of the lesson;

4 Sometimes feedback can cause a negative effect on a child's mood or indeed their learning;

5 Stickers and rewards are not feedback; they do not contain information about the task or indeed how to improve.

What is effective feedback?

1 Feedback needs to relate to the learning objective (LO);

2 There should be an expectation that the children you teach act on the feedback you have given – they need to be actively involved;

3 Feedback must be about learning not necessarily performance;

4 Feedback should never be personal but instead objective and focused on the task at hand;

5 Learning from mistakes is crucial (Growth Mindset);

6 Feedback should celebrate what the child has done well and achieved but also on what else the child needs to do to improve further;

7 In science, feedback should relate to the understanding of conceptual ideas and the honing of process skills.

We feel it important here to make a cautionary point about next-step marking. We have seen a growing trend in schools, especially in maths and English, to dogmatically insist that written next-step marking happens during and/or after every lesson. Not only does this add a huge amount of work to a busy classroom teacher's workload, it is not always effective or indeed necessary. Having said that, schools are now including this in marking policies and we feel it important that the readers of this book contemplate this.

Next-step marking

This can be thought of as a continuous process of formative assessment; next-step marking (sometimes referred to as intervention marking) can happen at any point of the lesson and can be used to give guidance, consolidation or challenge to the pupils that you teach; certainly, what you write should be meaningful and motivating; however, it is also important that this process of assessment is manageable to teachers.

Figure 7.2 Next-step marking of a year 5 child's work

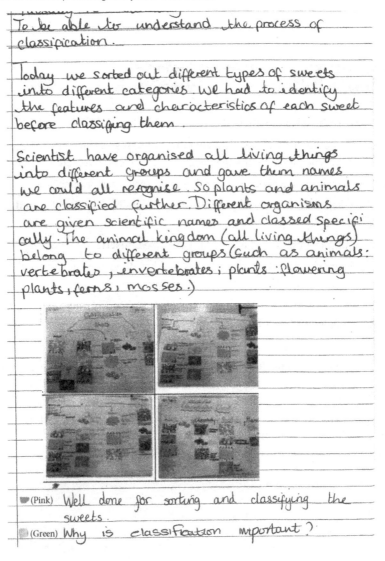

Figure 7.3 A year 6 child's work on micro-organisms

The micro-orginisms that break down dead plants animals matter are called decomposers. We also have special bacteria in our stomachs to help us digest food. Sometimes we eat heathly bacteria in yoghurts to help our digestion. (remember the yakult advert?)

(Pink)   You investigated micro organisms.
(Green) How does a virus spread?

Pause for thought

In both of these examples (7.2 and 7.3), the teacher has highlighted what the child has achieved in pink.

The next-step marking questions have been highlighted in green; reflect on the next-step questions in these examples and ask yourself:

- What is the teacher trying to achieve in terms of understanding of conceptual science?
- What process (enquiry) skills will the child need to use to complete the next-step marking?
- Do these questions consolidate understanding?
- Do they provide depth or challenge in science understanding?
- Are they motivational?
- Are they next-step marking questions?

Our thoughts on the examples above are as follows:

Figure 7.2:

- Pink – *'Well done for sorting and classifying the sweets.'*

  The teacher's feedback reflects the LOs and outcomes; however, there is no indication in the feedback of whether or not the classifying was correct.

- Green – *'Why is classification important?'*

  The next-step marking gives the child the opportunity to explain and justify, in his/her words, the functions of classification, thus deepening understanding.

Figure 7.3:

- Pink –'You have investigated micro-organisms.'

  This seems limited feedback. The teacher could have reflected on the scientific language used and the child's understanding of bacteria, decomposers etc.

- How does a virus spread?

  This gives the child an opportunity to explain the process or indeed use their research skills to find out about how a virus spreads, if they do not know; again, challenging the child while deepening their understanding.

Next-step marking – Our reflections:

1 Next-step marking can be a very effective way to enable children to progress in their knowledge and understanding of science.

2 In addition, next-step marking is a good opportunity for children to consolidate their understanding or indeed be challenged to develop their understanding using enquiry skills.

3 However, for the novice teacher, next-step marking can be very challenging. Teachers need a thorough knowledge of the curriculum, be able to ask effective questions and understand progression in science education; otherwise it will not be meaningful (designed to enhance performance and deepen understanding) and manageable.

4 If using next-step marking, teachers can plan this prior to the lesson (which is helpful for the novice teacher); however, they must also ensure that when planning the next lesson that this is designed to take into account the next steps given.

5 Marking does need to be manageable; however (see our points in Figure 7.3), in the long run, more detailed marking supports the class teacher when assessing the child and in understanding what they have achieved and what they need to focus on next. If the teacher had been more specific and detailed in their marking of 7.3, then when assessing the child's knowledge and understanding of micro-organisms, more detailed feedback will make assessment easier (for a start, the teacher won't need to read through all of the child's work again). Marking should inform both the child and the assessment made by the teacher of the child's knowledge, understanding and skills.

How is formative assessment/AfL recorded (monitoring over time)?

1 In the EYFS, formative assessment is recorded against the EYFS Profile (post-it notes, annotated plans etc).

2 KS1/2 – Simple grids/matrix recording whether the child/children have achieved the LO or learning intention (LI) and if not, the teacher can then record what barriers to learning exist – one way to achieve this is to compile evidence using a simple mark book.

3 Teachers should keep files of assessed work for evidence and moderation; this should include a variety of different formats, not only written work (more on this throughout this chapter)!

4 Ongoing assessment against age-related expectations (ARE) is now the expected norm in primary schools, which should be passed from year group to year group so that a profile for each child is built throughout their primary schooling which evidences their attainment and progress in science; this enables teachers to give a rich and robust picture of the scientific knowledge and understanding, as well as the process skills learnt, of each child – this is good practice as it reflects personalized, individualized provision; judgement is made on a range of activities and evidence rather than focusing on what children can simply achieve via tests!

How is summative assessment recorded (monitoring over time)?

1 EYFS Profile – continual formative assessment throughout the year provides reliable and accurate data about each child's level of development in order for teachers to make summative assessment judgements.

2 Pupil Progress Meetings – teachers are required to make summative judgements about their children's progress at several points throughout the year (ARE). Usually this is recorded via software such as Target tracker or SIMS – this enables teachers to monitor progress and attainment closely throughout the year and provide additional input where needed for children who have been identified as not making enough progress. All schools monitor progress of maths, reading and writing; with many now also monitoring science too.

3 Via end of year reports – reporting to parents.

4 Year 6 science sampling (SATS).

5   Moderation – your confidence and the confidence of the teachers you work with when assessing children's work can only be improved by regular moderation meetings across your year group, phase and school; as staff learn together what to look for. This also ensures that science maintains a high profile in schools and ensures that teachers have the evidence needed to make judgements about children's progress and attainment (summative assessment).

How much evidence is needed?

This is one of the first questions students ask us when assessing children's progress and attainment in science. Assessment in science should not be a tick box exercise. Still in some schools, teachers see assessment as ticking off targets (normally three times) as evidence that children have met their targets but this does not demonstrate robust understanding across the primary science curriculum. A range of assessment information from both group and individual work (written and oral) should feed into summaries of pupil progress; building profiles over time and across the primary age range. Therefore, evidence is not about how much but rather concerns quality of evidence which demonstrates progress and attainment.

Assessing working scientifically and process skills

As mentioned in Chapter 2, the assessment of scientific enquiry and the process skills needs to be better developed and a better balance between enquiry and concepts needs to be achieved. Some teachers, who might lack confidence in their own science understanding, find that the reliable assessment of the working scientifically strand of the National Curriculum can be challenging. If the school has a policy of 'evidence in the books', it can be problematic to plan and assess the children's progression in the 'doing of science'. By this we mean that too often, when visiting PGCE students, we have seen in schools where children's attainment in literacy and numeracy is low, science is used as a vehicle for more writing, rather than progression in enquiry skills. While this is worthy on some levels, and the scientific community does indeed need to communicate their results in written form, we suspect that this is not always the driver for the 'writing up' of science. In some cases, we have even observed that the success criteria include literacy criteria alongside some science concept, but nothing about the process of 'doing science'.

Subject knowledge is arguably the easiest aspect of learning science to assess. As Cross and Bowden (2014) argue, ask 5-year-olds to sing 'head, shoulders, knees and toes' and it will be self-evident which children can confidently label the body parts. The old Key Stage Two SATs were abandoned in 2009 because of the criticism that summatively assessing enquiry skills was not easy in a written test, and that in year 6, children were being drilled in the subject knowledge, in the way that, to be honest, many are today with literacy and numeracy. Of course, we all would agree that memory of facts does not necessarily show evidence of understanding, nor the application of the knowledge. Sadly, it appears that removing the testing at the end of KS2 has had the detrimental effect of science seeming to lose its status in many schools (CBI 2015), and particularly in those schools who have a focus on raising the achievement in literacy and numeracy. Consequently, in schools that lack confidence in science, and have a different agenda, the recommended two hours of science per week is not happening. In response to this alarming situation, the DFE, with the introduction of the revised curriculum in 2013, announced that there would be a 'science sampling' biennial programme with a random selection of schools, and a random selection of children in the year 6 cohort being required to sit tests in biology, physics and chemistry.

How have the new sampling tests overcome the difficulty of assessing the working scientifically strand via a written test, you may ask? Well, for example, as we write this, in the sample test materials for 2016, a section about the workings of the human body had one question that required the children to mark the position of the stomach on a diagram of the contents of the torso, and was the only one of the biology section which the mark scheme defined as coming under the working scientifically objectives thus:

> WS – Recording findings using simple scientific language, drawings, labelled diagrams, keys, bar charts and tables (DfE 2013).

Of course, there can only ever be questions about working scientifically based on presenting evidence, evaluating data (from graphs) and using scientific language, etc., but there is so much more to working scientifically than this. The guidance for the tests on the National Curriculum (2013) for science recognizes that it is not possible to assess children's understanding of choosing appropriate equipment, for example, or the setting up of tests and gathering data (KS2 Science Sampling Guidance 2016).

There is some evidence, however, that the narrowing of the curriculum in the way often seen does not in fact have the desired outcome: raised achievement in literacy and numeracy (Ward and Roden 2016:104). We don't find that hard to understand. If children are being subjected to this apparent narrowing of the curriculum, boredom and lack of engagement is a likely consequence, and it seems logical that disengagement will lead to poorer outcomes. Nevertheless, subject knowledge, at the end of a topic, say, can be easily 'tested' through written tasks, and the evidence is there for all to see. This might satisfy the leadership of the school in an accountability atmosphere, but, we would argue, have more to do with the teachers than the learners.

More challenging then, is the assessment of whether children are making progress in their understanding, confidence in and ability to take more ownership of 'Doing Science', of becoming increasingly scientific, of working like a scientist might work (Cross and Bowden 2014).

Planning for the development of enquiry skills

Before we can begin to think about reliable assessment, we science teachers need to think about what we are assessing in terms of the progress children are making in their enquiry skills.

Careful planning is required to ensure that there is a good balance over time of the different facets of the enquiry skills that need to be developed. The National Curriculum (2014) provides the information about what skills should be addressed in each year group to help you decide how you can get this balance. The effective science practitioner will ensure that they know the National Curriculum (2014) requirements very well indeed and not, as some of our PGCE students report, use only a bought in scheme of work or the plans produced by colleagues.

It follows that when planning for a unit of work in science, not only should there be objectives for the concepts, but also, in every session, there should be both objectives and success criteria for the process of doing science. How the teacher shares the LOs and success criteria with the children is much debated in research elsewhere (e.g. Ward and Roden 2016:102 and 2016:105), but 'not giving away the answer' to the concept being taught is easier if there is a focus on the process skills and the plenary of the lesson is used effectively to consolidate the concept.

So how can we as practitioners confidently and reliably assess the children's enquiry skills? After all, it is much easier to assess whether children have understood the concepts being taught. They both know and understand that magnets don't attract all metals, or they don't. The process skills are not so straightforward to assess. According to Ward and Remnant (2016), there are only three ways of gaining evidence about how the children are making progress:

- By observation
- Through discussion
- By marking work or looking at completed tasks

Let's consider these approaches. Given the discussion above about the challenges of reliably assessing children's process skills through written evidence, it would follow that the first two of the above strategies are the most appropriate for the assessment of the enquiry skills in the classroom environment, but let's think about the relative merits of each one.

Observation

It's all very well suggesting that observation will give you the evidence of children's developing enquiry skills, but in a busy classroom, you would be forgiven for wondering how you can capture what could be going on in one group of children while you are working with another. This can be achieved, however, with careful planning and rotating the groups of children you work with and focus on. By carefully planning the objectives for the process skills and making sure you are ready to notice when children achieve those objectives, the monitoring of your class and the children's progress in developing the skills will become manageable.

Figure 7.4 Children working together to complete an investigation

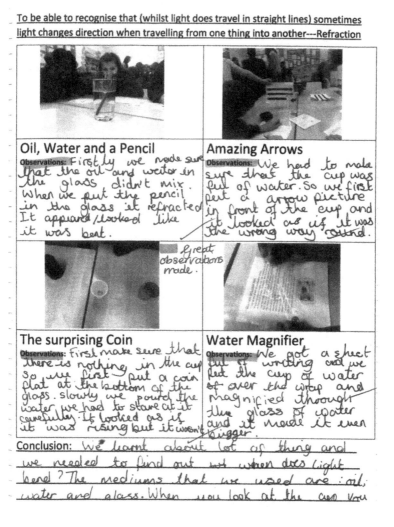

To be able to recognise that (whilst light does travel in straight lines) sometimes light changes direction when travelling from one thing into another---Refraction

Oil, Water and a Pencil
Observations: Firstly we made sure that the oil and water in the glass didn't mix. When we put the pencil in the glass it refracted. It appeared/looked like it was bent.

Amazing Arrows
Observations: We had to make sure that the cup was full of water. So we first put a arrow picture in front of the cup and it looked as if it was the wrong way round.

Great observations made.

The surprising Coin
Observations: First make sure that there is nothing in the cup. So we first put a coin flat at the bottom of the glass. slowly we poured the water we had to stare at it carefully. It looked as if it was rising but it wasn't.

Water Magnifier
Observations: We got a sheet full of writing and we put the cup of water over the wrap and magnified through the glass of water and it made it even bigger.

Conclusion: We learnt about lot of thing and we needed to find out when does light bend? The mediums that we used are : oil, water and glass. When you look at the cup you

Furthermore, a 'tuned in' practitioner will notice when children demonstrate a skill that is not your particular focus for that lesson or demonstrated by a child that is not in your focus group, and make a note of it straight away. Having a pad of sticky notes near you will enable you to write it down and date it, and this should begin to build up the evidence for children's progress in these all-important process and enquiry skills. It's how we used to do it in the EYFS before technology allowed us to capture the moments by photograph!

Through discussion

By 'listening in' to children's discussions about the enquiry they are engaged in, we can get very useful assessment information about their developing enquiry skills. Take the following excerpt of children's talk, for example:

CASE STUDY 7.1

Year 5 children talking about dissolving:

Child A: If we all have a go at stirring the mixture, that'll make it fair.

Child B: I'm not so sure, Sunil is stronger than me, so he might stir faster. Will that be fair?

Child C: I think we should just have one person, 'cos we're trying to find out if stirring makes the sugar disappear quicker, aren't we?

Child A: Well yes, but if it's between stirring and no stirring, how long do we stir, and does it make a difference if we all get to stir, say three times each?

What do these children understand about fair tests?

When working with your focus group, or focus children for that lesson, it's important that you have some pre-planned questions that you want to ask, so that you can make a note of the answers children give and thus assess their understanding of enquiry skills, and to promote more scientific thinking. It is the case that many of the questions teachers ask children are ones that require a right answer, and that as teachers, we probably have an idea of what answer we want. However, pre-planned questions need to be flexible and certainly open ended because the key to obtaining evidence for assessment purposes is to listen to the explanations and answers that children give. It's no good having a set of questions on the concept that are rattled off and sound like a test to the children; a 'guess what's in the teacher's head' type of question. It is the dialogic teaching (Alexander, 2017), the discussion between the child and the teacher, that will give rise to this evidence.

By looking at completed tasks

Where the policy of the school is to have evidence in the books, a strategy that is easy to manage is to use technology to collect this. Adopting the EYFS system of monitoring and recording using tablets or ipads is a good one and there are free apps that can be easily downloaded to assist you. Most schools nowadays have sets of tablets that can be 'booked' for your science lessons.

For example, if groups of children are engaged with an enquiry, what could be better than to give one child in the group of recording the particular LO associated with the process skills using pic-Collage for example, and capturing the practical stage of the investigation (gathering the data or information and presenting the results).

Similarly, by reflecting carefully on the kind of information that would tell you that children were learning and making progress in the process and enquiry

Figure 7.5 A diagram by a year 3 child observing how water is transported in a plant

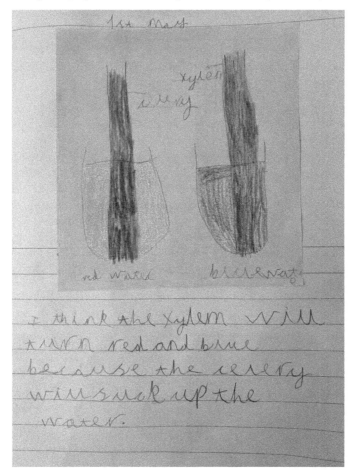

skills, it becomes easier to plan what you would like them to record in books. For example, an annotated drawing or diagram of their investigation will give useful evidence of whether a child had understood the purpose of observing over time, as the Figure 7.5 suggests.

What does the diagram tell us about the child's process skills? What more could we learn if we had a discussion with the child about her learning?

It may be that drawing conclusions and evaluating the enquiry could be done in written form in the books, which then is less of a difficulty for children who find writing a challenge than writing up the whole enquiry. All these activities, however, are evidence of children developing their enquiry and process skills.

Reporting to parents

As mentioned earlier, one of the important aspects of assessment is reporting attainment and progress to parents. Writing reports is an important skill to learn for the student teacher encompassing Past 2 of the Teachers' Standards as well as TS8.

CASE STUDY 7.2 – A report about end of year science attainment and progress

Henry pays attention in class and is keen to discuss his ideas with others. He likes science and puts forward his own ideas and suggestions about why things happen. His written work is clearly constructed and conveys his ideas well. He can use scientific symbols for electrical components and he labels diagrams when asked to. He records his findings in tables where appropriate. He links cause and effect in many of his explanations, which can sometimes be full and give a clear picture of what he has done. On occasions, Henry is able to make generalizations from his work but he needs assistance to interpret his results correctly. Sometimes, Henry gives partial explanations about his work and he sometimes misses out important details. Henry makes interesting links between things he notices in the environment and his work in science. Overall, Henry's work is satisfactory for his class but slightly below average for his year group (ARE).

Pause for thought

Take a look at the end of year report written about Henry's attainment and progress in science and then reflect on the following questions:

- Is the last sentence true?
- Is it useful?
- Will the child be disheartened?

- What does this report say about:
  - **a)** Henry's attainment in science, in relation to conceptual science and process skills?
  - **b)** Henry's progress in science?
- Does it imply that the class is below national standards?
- What do you think the reaction of his parents will be?
- Do you think it is possible to design a pro forma which can convey all this information more effectively?
- What would you keep from this report and what would you re-write?

CASE STUDY 7.3

Now, take a look at the following report for Deborah in year 5.

Achievement in Science

Science	Exceeding ARE	Meeting ARE	Below ARE
Knowledge and understanding	✓		
Working scientifically – process skills	✓		

Effort in Science

Science	Always works hard and is engaged	Usually works hard	Requires more motivation
Knowledge and understanding	✓		
Working scientifically – process skills	✓		

Science comment:

Deborah has demonstrated a good, solid understanding of the scientific ideas taught this year. She has been able to make scientific predictions based on her knowledge and understanding of science; and accurately record and explain her findings/data in various ways. She can accurately identify and name the main parts of the human circulatory system and describe the functions of the heart, blood vessels and blood. She has demonstrated that she understands that things have changed over time and that fossils provide living things that inhabited the Earth millions of years ago. She can explain the relationship between the brightness of a lamp or the volume of a buzzer, and the number and voltage of cells in the circuit.

Her hard work and effort is to be commended.

Next-step target

Deborah needs to understand and explain the importance of carrying out experiments numerous times (in relation to validity).

Pause for thought

- What are your initial thoughts about this report?
- What does it tell you about the child's achievement in relation to science?
- Is it ambiguous?
- Can it be improved?
- How would the child and parents feel about this report?

A final point – The TAPS project, Bath SPA University

The Teacher Assessment in Primary Science Project (TAPS) is a three-year project funded by the Primary Science Teaching Trust based at Bath Spa University; it's aim is to develop support for a valid, reliable and manageable system of science assessment which will have a positive impact on children's learning.

Working with schools, the project has looked at ways in which schools can use ongoing formative assessment; monitoring of pupil progress; summative reporting and whole-school reporting to provide a holistic view of assessment in primary science. We highly recommend that you read this important report on assessing in primary science as it will no doubt impact positively on your pedagogical understanding of assessment in science.

Summary

1 Assessment is a skill that student teachers need to develop and hone; it takes time to develop.

2 Assessment of progress and attainment is not a tick box exercise.

3 Teachers should build profiles of their children's progress and attainment over time which draws on all types of evidence, not simply written work.

4 AfL, formative assessment and summative assessment must form part of an assessment profile.

5 Moderation is an important part of teacher's confidence in assessing children's knowledge, understanding and process skills in science.

6 Feedback needs to be effective, following the principles set out in this chapter.

7 Report writing about science should report on scientific knowledge and understanding, process skills and effort/engagement.

Recommended reading

Brunton, P. and Thornton, L. (2012). *Science in the Early Years: Building Firm Foundations from Birth to Five.* Sage.

Christodoulou, D. (2016). *Making good progress? The Future of Assessment for Learning.* Oxford Press.

Clarke, S. (2014). *Outstanding Formative Assessment: Culture and Practice.* Hodder Education.

Harrison, C. and Howard, S. (2014). *Inside the Primary Black Box: Assessment for Learning in the Primary and Early Years Classrooms.* Learning Sciences International.

Nottingham, J. and Nottingham, J. (2017). *Challenging Learning through Feedback: How to get the type, tone and quality of feedback right every time.* Challenging Learning. https://pstt.org.uk/application/files/6314/5761/9877/taps-pyramid-final.pdf

Chapter 8
Practical Issues

You can know the name of a bird in all languages of the world, but when you're finished, you'll know absolutely nothing whatever about the bird ... so let's look at the bird and see what it is doing: that's what counts.

Carl Sagan

Chapter objectives

By the end of this chapter you will have an understanding of:

- How to plan effectively for science
- Issues relating to appropriate science equipment and resources
- How to use your additional adults to support science learning
- How Inclusion can be promoted in science
- How to challenge the children with high learning potential in your classroom

Introduction

The preceding chapters have examined why science learning is so vital for the development and well-being of our children and of society. This chapter explores some of the barriers to what we have put forward as effective primary science teaching and learning. We discuss some of the practical issues that may arise in the planning of and delivery of quality science experiences in the classroom that may not have a ready supply of resources, for example. It may be that your class demographics are such that you have a wide range of attainment among the children you teach, and that children are unused to working collaboratively with each other, and that you feel nervous of managing the excitement of practical science.

The inclusive nature of science is explored here, and some of the issues that might arise with fully inclusive learning in the classroom are discussed. We feel passionately that at its best, science can be accessible to all children at a level that is appropriate for individual children, and that all children can make progress in their scientific skills and understanding. If you take the view that the problem is not a child with learning difficulties, but a teacher with teaching difficulties, then a 'can-do' attitude will mean that all children can have access to the marvellous and exciting world of science.

What is important to consider when planning primary science?

Throughout this book, we have put forward the view that science is a vital subject for all children to be learning. It helps them explain the world around them, and all children can access well-planned science lessons at their own level. Planning for any subject is a crucial tool for the equitable coverage of the concepts and the skills, but as a core subject, science has a status that requires it be given very careful thought indeed. Not that we are advocating that other subjects need less careful planning, of course, but it is the particulars of science that we are discussing here. As we have seen in Chapter 6, maintaining children's curiosity and desire to find out things for themselves is of vital importance.

In long-term, school wide planning, a consideration needs to be given to the equitable balance between the physics, chemistry, biology and working scientifically strands of which the National Curriculum (2013) comprises. Additionally, there must be clear outline of the progression of science enquiry and the process skills. To this end, as discussed in the chapter on assessment, there should be a shared understanding of the age-related expectations among the staff, through a process of moderation of both concepts and skills. An overview of this balance needs to be undertaken by the science lead, with CPD for all members of staff (including additional adults working with children in the class room, which is discussed further later in this chapter). Remember that the current National Curriculum (2013) states what the children should know at the end of each year of study, but it doesn't tell the practitioner how to go about teaching it. Many primary teachers feel less confident about teaching the physics strand, and our own PGCE students' subject knowledge audit scores confirm this lack of confidence, so a careful monitoring of both the delivered and received curriculum for science should be in place.

Medium-term planning over the term and half term is often linked in with a topic in a cross-curricular way, but it is imperative that the science doesn't get lost or subsumed to the history or geography, say, and the integrity of the science skills and subject knowledge must be maintained. Some schools are now keeping science as a discrete subject in order to ensure the rigorous coverage is maintained. There is a tension that can arise in the planning of the medium-term plans in that if we are to start with the children's ideas, and continue to value their questions, then it is logical not to plan out all the lessons for the half term before the first session on the topic. Using the formative assessment techniques and strategies discussed in earlier chapters, we can elicit the children's ideas and indeed, what they would like to find out about in the topic. Thus, the medium-term planning should be flexible. Of course, no teacher is likely *not* to have planned out the skills and enquiries the topic is likely to engender over the medium term. This must be done to ensure progression in both concepts and skills. However, this should be a reasonably loose framework in order to start where the children in the class are, in the best social-constructivist tradition. This is where the effective teacher needs to be certain of subject knowledge and how the National Curriculum expects children to learn; from the children's ideas, can the topic be planned.

For the short-term planning of individual lessons, the important thing here is the children's previous assessment for learning. Among the four principles for assessment identified by Black and Harrison (2004: 4), we find that the first principle is that planning should 'start from where the learners are, as learners have to be active in reconstructing their ideas'. Thus, through evaluations of previous lessons, the reflection on the evidence from 'doing' science and the marking of completed tasks, the science teacher will have formulated the next steps for both individuals and the whole class. From this assessment for learning, teachers will be able to decide which groups of children work together and what support needs to be given. This is discussed in more detail later in this chapter in the sections on inclusion and working with the additional adults in the classroom, if any.

It is not our intention here to discuss in detail how to plan a lesson: different schools have different ways of doing this, but if you are a trainee teacher, or recently qualified, we would recommend some particular aspects of teaching science in the primary classroom that you could consider, in order to have successful science sessions with your children.

First, we would suggest that you are careful when planning for enquiry that you don't 'give away the answer' in your learning objectives. What we mean is, think about what it means for the learning objective to be couched as an 'I can' statement that describes the activity, rather than the learning. This is when it is imperative to have a process or enquiry objective alongside a concept one.

Pause for thought

Consider the difference between these two objectives:

'I can explain that plants need sunlight to be healthy'

compared with

'I can explain what plants need to be healthy'.

Which one has the scope for allowing children to find out for themselves?

The first one straight away implies that a child can be told that sunlight is needed for photosynthesis, and so have that knowledge, and if you're lucky, remember it. The second objective implies that some investigation has occurred wherein the child has had to find out what conditions plants need for healthy growth, evaluate what their observations tell them, and to be able to understand enough about the issue to be able to explain it to someone else. That seems much more satisfying to us, and in the constructivist tradition of Piaget (1961), children are making sense of the phenomenon through their own experiences. Figure 8.1 gives ideas of how you might word your learning objectives for both concepts and skills using Bloom's

Figure 8.1 Writing Learning Objectives using Bloom's Taxonomy

Key Words for Writing Learning Objectives linked to Bloom's Taxonomy

Progression in Bloom's Taxonomy	Child is able to/will learn to:	Key Words to use in Learning Objectives or Success Criteria
Comprehension	• Rephrase an idea • Put a definition in own words • Explain or summarize	Compare; contrast; sort; classify; categorize; find; sequence; order; rephrase; relate; organize; review; illustrate; indicate; question; suggest; clarify; explain; represent; discuss; consider
Application	• Use knowledge learned to find solutions to problems • Make generalizations	Link; predict; present; select; choose; compose; generalize; demonstrate; solve; calculate; control; illustrate; investigate; check; construct; design; devise; develop; plan; improvise; interpret; apply; check; make; produce; search
Analysis	• Decide what knowledge needs to be used to find out or solve problems by analysing parts of the problem – focus is to 'find out why'	Analyse; solve; conclude; separate; challenge; discover; criticize; distinguish; interpret
Synthesis	• Put together the parts of something to form something new	Combine; improvise; perform; formulate; compose; derive; create; reconstruct; review
Evaluation	• Use careful and considered judgements to make a decision	Evaluate; determine; deduce; support; defend; argue; criticise; assess; justify; judge; appraise; resolve

Key Words for Writing Learning Objectives linked to Bloom's Taxonomy

Skills and Attitudes for Learning Objectives

Attitudes	Share; participate; respect; reflect; co-operate; value; persevere; appreciate; improvise; collaborate; accept
Communication	Listen; express; perceive; support; present; clarify; represent; develop; argue; quality; justify; display; reason; discuss; oppose; perform; comment; inform; tell; show
Response	Question; answer; respond; convey; contribute; memorize; differentiate; visualize; evaluate; examine; write; store; retrieve; repeat; transfer; collect; decide; review; generate; construct; consider; investigate; explore; appraise; experiment; enter; process; create; produce; prepare; distinguish; follow
Practical Skills	Cut; shape; measure; estimate; weight; count; time; draw; construct; join; control

Taxonomy as a starting point, and indeed for differentiation, without 'giving the game away'.

Secondly, think carefully about your assessment for learning. As discussed in the chapter on assessment, plan for what you will see or hear that will tell you that learning has been achieved. Incorporate these into your success criteria so that when you see the evidence, you are ready to record it. This is easier to do if you feel secure about your subject knowledge and pedagogical content knowledge. Do your research thoroughly before you begin to teach a particular topic, so you are confident that you know both what you are teaching and what to expect of the children in terms of their naïve ideas and common misconceptions. This way, you won't find yourself at a loss when children ask left of field questions you're not too sure about. You'll be able to confidently deal with these without giving away any answers, but by suspending judgement and coming back to them sometime later and asking if the children now had any different ideas.

One other important aspect of planning for science, particularly when you are just beginning your teaching career, is to meticulously plan strategies to manage the excitement that doing the practical aspects of science brings about. Many teachers we see in schools are understandably nervous of what might seem to be a less 'structured' session, and worry about the management of excited children. Children should be excited about practical work, of course, and where they are excited, often learning is enhanced. Children remember the more practical experiences of the primary learning, and often when we ask our PGCE students what science do they remember from their primary days, it is the exciting 'wow' lessons that stand out in their memories. What we would say to you if you are a bit anxious about having groups of children engaged in enquiries and using equipment, is that the more you do it, the more you will see your young scientists purposefully engaged in their learning. So even if your first attempts at practical enquiries in the classroom seem a bit chaotic, don't be put off; keep on doing it! By the way, so that you are not left with clearing away all the equipment at the end of the afternoon, be sure to train your class to clear away, and clean if necessary, the equipment they have used.

When planning for any kind of practical science in your classroom, you must be rigorous in your approach to health and safety and the risks that might be involved. Don't be alarmed because I've just used the word 'risk'! Children need practice at handling situations that are a bit more risky than sitting at a desk, writing, and if they don't have exposure to 'managed' risks, are unable to make their own risk assessment later in life.

Luckily, there is much advice to help you in this and to ensure that you feel completely secure in what you need to put in place, and what practices you need to insist on with the children so that they are kept safe and feel confident that they can safely work scientifically. By year 5, children who have had plenty of opportunity to do practical science should be able to manage heating and melting using tea lights perfectly sensibly and safely. Having said that, we were once working with a group of PGCE students on reversible and irreversible changes, and didn't occur to us that adults would be unaware of the risk involved in putting a finger into melted sugar!

The Association for Science Education has a wonderful and much recommended book called 'Be Safe' which when consulted will reveal exactly how such equipment can be managed safely on group tables in the classroom. Furthermore, it will let you know which chemicals are safe to use at primary level, and give very useful information on taking children outdoors to use their local environment for science enquiry. This will make your risk assessment that much more secure. Practical advice on safety issues in the classroom can also be gained from accessing the CLEAPSS (The Consortium of Local Authorities for the Provision of Science Services) website (address at the end of the chapter).

One other thing to remember when planning for your science practical lessons is to ensure that the equipment you need is in good working order. Always check in good time that if, for example, you are going to be exploring electrical circuits with your children, that alongside enough crocodile leads, the light bulbs or buzzers are in good working order and that you have enough new batteries for the circuits to work. Similarly, check that all the magnets are working if you are learning about magnetism. Magnets that are knocked about too much lose their attraction!

Figure 8.2 is an example of the detail of a successful science plan, which draws on questions and ideas that the children had, and is kindly given to us by a teacher who studied with us some years ago.

What should I do about the lack of equipment in my school?

One of the reasons teachers give as to why they do not do as much practical enquiry-based science is whether they will be able to organize enough resources for the practical work. Similarly, some argue that it takes such a long time to hunt around in the dusty old science cupboard for hours trying to find the resources and equipment they will need. These are valid reasons to give in some schools where perhaps science doesn't have the status of the other core subjects, and there has been no budget, even for consumables, afforded to the science lead for some time.

However, anecdotally we can report that things might be about to get better! With the random biennial science sampling beginning to roll out for year 6 pupils, school leadership is beginning to wake up to the idea that science needs to be taught effectively throughout the school, and the National Curriculum (2013) is clear that a range of different enquiry types needs to be taught in each year group. Our PGCE students and the School Direct Salaried (SDS) students report an upturn in CPD in schools and more regular moderation of the science provision. If the working scientifically strand is to be delivered effectively, then equipment needs to be accessible, and there needs to be enough of it to allow the children to participate in enquiries. This would suggest an increased budget allocated to the subject in order to provide for the requirements of classes of children.

Figure 8.2 Example of successful science planning – with thanks to Clapham Manor Primary School

Science Plan

Topic: Materials/ scientific enquiry   **Class:** 5   **Teacher:**   **Term:** Summer 2

Week beginning: w.c. 11.04.16

From previous learning:
- Plan different types of scientific enquiry to answer questions, including recognising variables.
- Recording data/ results of increasing complexity using scientific diagrams, labels, classification keys, tables, scatter graphs, bar/ line graphs.
- Reporting and presenting findings from enquiries including conclusions, explanations, and relationships – oral and written.
- Identify scientific evidence that has been used to support/ refute ideas/ arguments.

Knowledge from NC:
- compare and group together everyday materials on the basis of their properties, including their hardness, solubility, transparency, conductivity (electrical and thermal), and response to magnets
- give reasons, based on evidence from comparative and fair tests, for the particular uses of everyday materials, including metals, wood and plastic

New Learning/Outcomes: (from medium term plans)
Writing opportunities: cross curricular links:

	New Learning / Outcomes	What's going to be assessed? How is it going to be assessed? [Progress Checks]	Organisation - Activities, Resources, Differentiation	Review/Evaluation (not achieved/ exceeded)	Vocabulary
1 Day/Date	<u>Compare and group everyday materials on their basis of their properties.</u> <u>Present findings in an effective way.</u>	Can ch. discuss compare/ contrast materials using up levelled sophisticated vocabulary? Write a dictionary definition for material (Vocabulary showcase) Can you justify your explanations? What properties could you see? If you zoomed in/ used a microscope what would wood/ cotton wool look like? How would they be different?	*Warm up: What's better a chair made of cotton wool or a teapot made out of chocolate? (Talking chips).* Ink Waster/ vocab work – predict meaning of scientific vocab. Give meanings/ Ipads – up level definitions. Collaborative learning: sorting everyday materials. Devise own categories – buzzer every 10 mins. Photograph different ways/ post it explanations. Writing frame/ vocabulary to support explanations. U&A – choose 3 materials for your desert island – rate out of 10 and give a reason why.		**Hardness** **Soft** **Solid** **Transparency** **Conductivity** **Solubility** **Insoluble** **Opaque** **Magnetic** **Thermal** **Conductor** **Insulate**
2	Use a variety of sources to explore suitability of materials to purpose. <u>To read for meaning/ use strategies to read non-fiction.</u>	**Canvas V Lightweight?** **How will it adapt to different conditions?** **How will it be transported there?** **Cost?**	<u>Introduce problem –</u> 120,000 refugees without homes – What's the solution? Mind map ideas. Write 3 solutions.		**Durable** **Rigid** **Non-flammable** **Light weight.**

Science Plan

	Can you summarise what you have read? **How could present this to someone in a different way?** **Q&A?** **Vocabulary/ Frayer – choose a material. (To ensure understanding from reading)**	Watch clip – uplevel. Analyse photos (draw diagrams) of refugee shelters. Properties of materials used/ why? Compare/ contrast, rate effectiveness – how do the materials suit conditions. What are the conditions in Syria? Reading – non-fiction about properties of different plastics/ fabric (home learning) http://www.unhcr.org/pages/49c364 6cf2.html http://www.dezeen.com/2013/07/0 3/Ikea-develops-flat-pack-refugee-shelters/ http://www.bbc.co.uk/schools/gcseb itesize/design/graphics/materialsand componentsrev3.shtml Can you compete with Ikea? How?
3	Reporting and presenting findings from enquiries – explanations. Using information from reading/ research to present in an appropriate way.	**Organise concept map accordingly?** **Group materials according to properties?** **Can children spot similarities and differences between plastics/ canvas?** **Fabric isn't strong – agree/ disagree.** *How does metal look different to fabric?* *Why are there similarities and differences?*	*Warm up – Concept cartoon – materials* *Zoom in – what does fabric look like under a microscope* *https://msnucleus.org/membership/ html/k-6/as/scimath/6/assm6_8d.html* *Diagram- prediction/ uplevel after looking at scientific images.* *Create concept map of materials for refugee shelters – use text/ Ipads to support research – concept map should show relationships between materials and include explanations – this will be used when designing shelter.* *As a group – choose materials to test*

(Continued)

Figure 8.2 Continued

Science Plan

		– you must rate and give reasons for these choices.
4 Plan different types of scientific enquiry to answer questions, including recognising variables. **Fair testing** **Recording** **Data collection**	**Why is timing important in making the testings fair? What are the variables? Control, independent, dependent?** **Refer to previous learning.** **Why will averages/ mean be important?** **Predictions?** **Hypothesis – difference between?**	**Warm up - A solid can never be described as soft – agree or disagree. (from marking)** **Planning testing:** Ch. have to plan/ devise way of testing water resistance/ heat resistance/ durability. How to record this? Focus on fair testing? (give scenarios to refute this) **Devise way of recording/ data collection.** **HOT BOARD QUESTION PACKS – challenge.**
5 • Recording data/ results of increasing complexity using scientific diagrams, labels, classification keys, tables, scatter graphs, bar/ line graphs. • Collaborative learning		**Testing materials** **Health and Safety** **Recording**

What's heavier a ton of feathers or a ton of bricks
A solid can never be described as soft - agree of disagree.
Is a solid always hard – prove/ disprove?

Notes from pupil voice 21.04.16
Science – materials unit

Concept map about materials – uses of materials A3.   Science reading text/ Ipads
Test the materials out – test which ones are waterproof, test heat, samples and record these, set the materials – safety – the fire triangle,

Science Plan

Making the tents – make things outside – 3 x different groups and different materials, use the skills from camping, test whether it's heat proof, water proof, test durability, electric fan, choose the best, making some models, strength of fabrics,

Metal, plastic, wood – put it in the sun, put it in the freezer.

Spinney.

Diagrams of shelters – scientific vocabulary, materials,

Man Made V Natural

Writing opportunities:

Information text about materials.

News paper report on the discovery of a new material.

Write about the past and who invented plastic.

Write to the refugees to explain how we are helping.

Write a persuasive letter for people to help.

Persuasive letter to the government –

A diary entry as one of the refugees.

Government/ community – to say what materials are suitable to make the shelters.

http://www.bbc.co.uk/news/resources/idt-841ebc3a-1be9-493b-8800-2c04890e8fc9

So, if you find that the science resource cupboard in your school doesn't have the equipment you need when you are planning your science provision, you should bring this to the attention of your science lead, and ask him or her to purchase what you need. It goes without saying that to do this, you will need to plan your topic and the enquiries and process skills you might develop in advance and with enough time to procure the equipment you will need. In your medium-term planning, while allowing for children's ideas to take the lead, you will have hopefully researched the age-related expectations for the enquiries likely to be appropriate for the topic, so you will have a good idea in advance what equipment you are likely to need. It's worth noting though, that many of the investigations that the children are likely to be carrying out for the chemistry strand of the curriculum require equipment, materials and chemicals that can be brought from the supermarket or the local pound shop very cheaply, so be resourceful, and if you find that you have had to make a shopping trip in order to deliver your science lessons, keep the receipt and claim expenses!

How can I effectively deploy staff in primary science?

Blatchford et al. (2008) undertook research into the impact of additional adults on children's learning, and found that TAs have a very positive impact on the behaviour in primary classrooms generally, but surprisingly had very little impact on children's progress with the learning. In other words, being supported by the TA doesn't necessarily help to 'close the gap' between lower achieving children and their peers. This finding doesn't seem yet to have impacted on practice in many classrooms, where TAs are still regularly found to be scaffolding the learning of usually the lower achieving children in the class. As practitioners, most teachers find the additional adult working in the classroom with them to be a very positive and welcome practice. So, how can we make the most effective use of any additional adults in the classroom? In part, it is to do with how the science is organized in your classroom, and this has implications for your inclusive practice that is discussed more in the next section. The Education Endowment Foundation (EEF) has helpfully used Blatchford et al.'s (2008) recommendations to put together some advice on this, and whether your classroom is arranged with 'ability' groups or mixed-ability groups, the advice is sound.

Most of the advice rests with the need to be able to have good communication with your additional adult so that they feel part of the teaching and learning process. According to the EEF, teachers should ensure, either through discussion or through detailed planning that is shared, that the TA has the essential information about how the lesson will unfold. So, they will need to know what are the concepts, facts or information being taught; what skills need to be learnt, applied, practised or extended; what the intended learning outcomes are and what is expected or required of the learners.

In our opinion, it is the last piece of advice that is the one that is sometimes difficult for TAs to gauge. We say this because, it seems to us that if the TA always works with the same group of children, and in many cases this will be the lower attaining group of children in the class. (One colleague told us recently she had come across a class where this group was known as the 'snails' group – make of that what you will!) If that is the case in your class, then it is difficult for the TA to have an understanding of these 'expectations', as they possibly don't get to experience what the other children are doing or producing. If you can give your TA the opportunity to move a round the groups of children, it also gives you the chance to work, and therefore assess, the children in the lower achieving groups, and be able to effectively plan next steps for them. It is very clear in the Teaching Standards (2012) that all teachers are expected to provide for all the children in the class.

Pause for thought

- What is the situation with the deployment of the TA in your class?
- Does the TA always support the lower achieving children?
- How will you know what the lower achieving children can do in science?

Above all, we should be encouraging our TAs to have high expectations of all the children in the class, and as such we need to be aware that some TAs are more concerned with the task being 'completed', so may find themselves giving more help to the children they work with than is necessary (Blatchford et al. 2008). This can lead to a situation where the children develop a lack of confidence in themselves and a 'learned helplessness' whereby the children do not believe they can manage any task on their own. By ensuring that your TA understands what you want the children to achieve on their own, through lots of discussions about your expectations, this can be ameliorated.

How can inclusion be promoted in science?

Many student teachers as well as those at the beginning of their career find the idea of practical science for children who have additional needs quite daunting. The idea of differentiating a practical task, or planning an investigation seems impossible. The range of children in any classroom who have some barriers to learning can seem overwhelming in our need to personalize the learning for them. However, we believe primary science to be one of the most inclusive subjects we teach, if it is done effectively. By taking part in the practical activities, children who find learning that bit harder in literacy and maths, or who find their behaviour difficult to manage can often shine when engaged in group work of a practical nature. Groups planning and doing an enquiry together and other collaborative tasks can allow all children to access the learning at their own level.

One for the first decisions you, as a teacher, will need to consider when planning for all children to be able to access the science will be whether you want to organize the groups as 'mixed-ability' groups or as groups of children whose learning needs are similar: the ability groups.

One of the advantages for children's learning in science of the mixed-ability groupings is that it gives ample opportunity for children's talk, which we have seen in Chapter 4 is so important for developing thinking skills and problem-solving. It draws on the opportunity for children to peer scaffold the learning for each other, and for Vygotsky's (1978a, b) idea of the More Knowledgeable Other to be a peer rather than an adult. According to Black and Wiliam (1998) peers are able to accept feedback from peers and take more notice of it, than they ever do of the feedback from adults, so it seems logical to capitalize on this, and allow them to encounter the peer-led learning. This also gives the teacher the opportunity to 'eavesdrop' on the conversations and discussions going on in the group, and assess each pupil in the group for that more difficult to assess aspect of science: the 'working scientifically' strand.

A further advantage to the mixed-ability grouping is that it is more inclusive for those children than perhaps in English and maths. In the so-called 'morning groups', some children who have barriers to learning, those who have English as an additional language and those who have behaviour difficulties, are often given less opportunities to interact with their peers in the other groups, and also may well be supported by the TA. This regular support can in itself be a barrier to social inclusion since the adult is so often 'in the way' of children talking to one another.

Children for whom English is an additional language will have their language development enhanced by hearing the rich discussions of the higher achieving children and, of course, the assumption that those who are new to English can't do the science is a mistake. With appropriate support, such as dual language vocabulary cards, and using scientific vocabulary in context and with pictures and diagrams to support understanding, children for whom English is an additional language will have the opportunity to access the science learning that much better. There is some evidence, too, that the ability grouping can actually set children up to fail, as it can create low expectations and a divisive element in the classroom community (Boaler 2009).

It is also very important to be sensitive to the different needs of children in the class in other ways. Valuing difference is an important element of our practice in schools, and a little careful thought can save us from inadvertently excluding some children. If, for example, you are teaching year 5 about healthy diet, and decide that a good way to enhance that would be for children to design and cook healthy pizzas in the school pizza oven (yes, some schools do have these in their grounds!), it is wise not to do this during the month of Ramadan. If you have Muslim children in your class, you will know that many of them begin to fast for Ramadan at this age, and thus to plan for such an exciting lesson at this time would be to exclude some of your children.

Similarly, since the National Curriculum (2013) states that we should be now teaching children about famous scientists, you do not need to only use the examples given in the non-statutory guidance. Be sensitive again to the diversity of the children in your class and choose a good range of female scientists, scientists from a range of ethnicities, and more modern scientists to excite and draw children in so that they see the relevance to their own lives. If you're learning about space, why not refer to Dr Maggie Aderin-Pocock, the black astrophysicist who has presented *The Sky at Night* for the past four years. Modern scientists who are leading the way in exciting new discoveries such as Vantablack, a material that absorbs so much light that you can't see objects in 3D, would take the learning that much further if you were learning about light in year 6, and the Royal Society of Chemistry has wonderful resources and ideas for including Islamic Scientists (among other topics) in your teaching in the primary science resources section on their website.

Table 8.1 An example of dual language vocabulary cards, that are easily made using a translating tool from the internet. These ones are English to Polish

Force	nauki
Push	Pchać
Pull	Ciągnąć
Friction	tarcie
Faster	szybciej
Slower	Wolniej

Figure 8.3 A photo of Vantablack nanotubes being grown on foil

As we said earlier, science practical work can give children the opportunity to shine and develop confidence in ways that English and maths may not. Consider the case study below and reflect on its implications to practice.

Pause for thought

One of our PGCE students was working with a group of children in year 6 on a task of three consecutive lessons with the focus working scientifically. The class teacher always had the children in their 'literacy' groups for science, but the student asked for a mixed-ability group to work with. The student reported that one girl who was considered very high achieving was uncomfortable and began to disengage with the conversations about planning the enquiry, while a child who was usually supported by the TA was confidently talking about the processes they would need to go through to make the enquiry a fair test.

The student discussed this with the class teacher later, and together they came to the conclusion that the high achieving child who always got everything she did 'right' was uncomfortable because the task was open ended and involved an element of problem-solving. She had been used to doing well because her written work was always of a high standard, but she hadn't developed a 'growth mindset' (Dweck 2017), discussed in Chapter 1. This child seemed not to have developed perseverance and a willingness to engage with the unknown, which is so important for doing science.

On the other hand, the child who found literacy difficult, and was usually supported by the TA for science, had had good scaffolding over time, and was confident in understanding what needed to be thought about in planning an enquiry.

Food for thought?

The challenge for us as teachers is to reflect carefully on what we mean by challenging the high achievers when it comes to science. As the above example shows, it is not enough to keep children in their ability 'morning' groups and think that because they do more quality writing about the concepts we are teaching, that they are also high achieving scientists.

'Gifted and Talented', 'High Attainers' or the 'More Able'?

In the above section of this chapter, we have given you *food for thought* when it comes to expectations for providing high-quality provision for all and argued that it is important to realize that all children have barriers to learning and personalized needs, it's just that some are simply more visible than others!

The framework document for the national curriculum in England: Key stages 1 and 2 (2013: 7) states that teachers have *'an even greater obligation to plan lessons for pupils who have low levels of prior attainment'* or who, indeed, are from *'disadvantaged backgrounds'*; high expectations should be set *'for every pupil'*. This might seem daunting for you as a novice teacher but be reassured that setting suitable challenge for the pupils we teach is in fact a challenge for all teachers; but not one that is impossible to meet.

We turn now to the directive for the national curriculum framework that teachers should **'plan stretching work for pupils whose attainment is significantly above the expected standard'** (2013: 8) – therefore, what does significantly above the expected standard mean? In order to understand this, we need to take a look at the language and definitions surrounding this.

Definitions?

There are a number of definitions relating to provision for pupils whose attainment is significantly above the expected standard which you need to be aware of.

The first is 'Gifted and Talented' which was a term used by schools to describe children who have the **potential** to develop significantly beyond what is expected of their age in one or more of the domains of human ability: intellectual, creative, social and physical; talented refers to children having skills above average in one or more areas of human performance (Gagne 1999) or in relation to identification of those who are 'Gifted and Talented', schools have been guided by the DCFS (2008), who state that gifted and talented refers to *'children and young people with one or more abilities (or skills in relation to talented) developed to a level significantly ahead of their year group or with the potential to develop those abilities'* (2008: 1). In 2012, the Sutton Trust recommended that *'the confusing and catch-all construct gifted and talented be abandoned'* and suggested that schools should instead be concerned with excellence in school subjects, which they termed as **'highly able'**.

More recently, the Ofsted Inspection Framework (2015) focuses on pupils deemed **'Most Able'** (NACE 2016), but do not set a definition of **'Most Able Pupils'**. Where applicable, Ofsted typically adhere to definitions set by the DfE (2013); however, in this case they also state that there is no national definition of the term **'Most Able'** (DfE 2013) but it is certainly the term now adopted by all schools. In addition, as the **'More Able'** refers to **potential**; therefore, the phrase **'Higher Attainers'** is used by Ofsted (2015) in relation to performance tables as it is related directly to what has actually been achieved.

Personally, we agree with Potential Plus (formally the Association of Gifted Children) who prefer the term **'high learning potential'**; we both find the term **'Able'** in itself derisive with the potential to negatively label children's **potential** – it certainly goes against Dweck's (2006) notion of a 'growth mindset'. There is a danger that it can be interpreted by some as having an underlying incorrect assumption that only those who are able can achieve, or on the contrary, that the 'More Able' do not need provision as they can easily achieve or are not at risk of underachievement – nothing could be further from the truth:

> Sometimes those with high abilities in one or more areas of learning may also suffer from a disability or difficulty in others. This can present a considerable barrier to the achievement of **potential**, as well as leading to frustration and disaffection. Developing strategies and approaches to countering underachievement should be an integral part of the school policy. (DfE 2008: 4)

Therefore, how do schools now define the 'More Able' and how does this relate to provision in science?

In terms of data, the '*Most Able*' are identifiable at KS1 as having made an Average Point Score (APS) of more than 18 points; and 30 points or more at KS2 in English and/or maths. It is important to note that unlike providing for children with SEND or EAL, there is no requirement to have a specific 'More Able Registry' or a 'More Able Policy' in schools although NACE (2016) considers it to be good practice.

With the removal of assessment levels when assessing children's progress and attainment, a school's internal tracking systems, along with the school's context, should also be used to define and identify the 'Most Able' children in the school. Before reading Tables 8.2 and 8.3, please complete and reflect on the questions in the following pause for thought:

Pause for thought

- How does your school define and identify, significantly above the expected standard, in Science?
- What does this look like in terms of data?
- Is this the same definition for English and maths?
- What general characteristics, do you think, a child who is 'More Able' might have?
- What characteristics might a child who is 'More Able' in science exhibit?

As you can see from Tables 8.2 and 8.3, there are many ways in which children can exhibit the characteristics of being 'More Able' and in particular in science. Of course, children do not need to exhibit all of these characteristics; your job as the class teacher is to look for, recognize and identify your children who are 'More Able' in science and provide work which stretches and challenges them so that they can reach their '*full potential!*'.

Table 8.2 Possible characteristics of a 'More Able' child (DfE 2008; NACE 2016)

• Asks a lot of questions, asks searching questions	• Interested in adult themes and issues
• Thinks quickly	• Enjoys setting problems
• Understands complex instructions	• Has a vivid/unusual imagination
• Grasps new concepts easily; remembers and applies them	• Often has strong opinions
• Has a thirst for knowledge	• Loses interest when asked to do more of the same
• Has wide vocabulary and talked early	• May read early
• Makes perceptive, original comments	• A high oral ability but poor writing skills
• Relates well to adults	• Uses conceptual understanding to make abstract links
• Becomes frustrated when unable to do something easily	• Responds extremely positively to new challenges – enjoys challenging work (seeking multiple answers and accepting that there might not be one right answer)
• Actively seek out new challenges	
• Might be keen to disguise his/her abilities	• Be self-taught; know more than you about a particular subject
• Could have behavioural abilities	

Table 8.3 Possible characteristics of a 'More Able' child in science

• Demonstrates strong curiosity about objects and environments; to seek explanations for the things and events they observe, often asking many questions, especially 'Why?'	• Can detect flaws in reasoning of others (and own)
	• Can hypothesize readily, manipulate variables fairly and make predictions
• Shows interest in collecting, sorting, and classifying objects	• Can suggest a variety of alternative strategies for testing predictions or gathering evidence
• Demonstrates (and sustain) high interest in investigating scientific phenomena	• Is able to perceive rapidly the direction of an investigation and anticipate outcomes
• Demonstrates intense interest in one particular area of science (e.g. space physics) to the exclusion of other topics.	• Can identify patterns in data where the links are not obvious
• Shows strong powers of concentration	• Is able to quantify experimental results by counting, weighing or otherwise measuring
• Can be easily bored by over-repetition of basic ideas but enjoy challenges and problem-solving	• Can produce models – they may model mathematically
• Has the tendency to make observations and ask perceptive questions	• Can generate creative and valid explanations
• Can learn novel ideas readily: they can quickly understand models and theories	• Is able to use a more extensive scientific vocabulary than their peers when explaining things and events
• Can relate novel ideas to familiar ones, including the ability to make connections between scientific concepts and observed phenomena	• Can reflect on their own thinking and learning
	• Can take on roles and exercise leadership within a group/investigation
• Is prepared to live with uncertainty	• Copes well with abstract aspects of science, linking conceptual understanding to abstract concepts
• Perseverance is high	• Likely to have developed greater metacognitive knowledge (knowledge of their own thinking and learning skills)
• Possibly know more about a topic in science than peers or the teacher	

Table 8.4 An example of a comment made by a 'More Able' child in science when thinking about scientific concepts in the real world

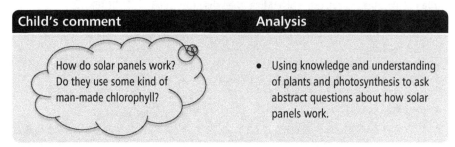

Child's comment	Analysis
How do solar panels work? Do they use some kind of man-made chlorophyll?	• Using knowledge and understanding of plants and photosynthesis to ask abstract questions about how solar panels work.

What can you do to provide for the more able in science lessons?

There are some great resources on the market (Hymer and Hailstone 2009; Tunnicliffe 2010; Gershon 2016) to enable you to provide for the 'Most Able' in your classroom.

Principles in provision for the 'More Able' in science should include:

- Create an ethos where being bright and enjoyed is 'VALUED'.
- Give pupils a choice in selecting activities and approaches they use.
- Encourage all pupils to become independent learners and self-study (where appropriate).
- Rich questioning – use Bloom's Revised Taxonomy (Anderson and Krathwohl 2001) or indeed SOLO Taxonomy (Biggs and Collis 1982) to challenge pupils further in their higher-order and abstract thinking (handling ambiguity and paradox).
- Make thinking explicit: learners should be asked to be explicit when using inductive and deductive reasoning: being encouraged to cite evidence, or sources of hunches, and explain the logic used in drawing conclusions. Teaching can model appropriate thinking strategies for students.
- Development of advanced scientific language skills, to include accuracy, precision and fluency.
- Transfer of knowledge across disciplines – linking ideas across topic and fields, this encourages analysis skills; for example, ask children to categorize information from a series of lessons.

- Provision of leadership opportunities – provide group work which enables children to take on different roles (remember to use Vygotsky's 1978, idea of the More Knowledgeable Other).

- Curriculum enrichment – breadth and depth is key, do not give children more of the same – individualized learning is the key, and specifically planned for.

Enquiry and the 'More Able':

- Provide open-ended tasks and questions to encourage creative and critical thinking, for example if you had used a different material/solution in this investigation what might have happened and why?; if Marie Curie had known about the danger she had put herself in, would she have continued to work with radium?; can you come up with a question to research that I (the teacher) don't know the answer to?

- Problem-based learning: enquiry allows students to investigate authentic problems, in 'real-world' contexts (as discussed in Chapter 5), and so can motivate able students who may become genuinely interested in finding answers and solutions.

- Design: experimental design allows students to demonstrate creativity, as well as apply logical thinking.

- Drawing conclusions: enquiry provides opportunities for children to draw their own conclusions, identifying patterns and making generalizations.

- Enquiry skills – encourage children to record data in different ways, or produce mathematical models where appropriate.

- Appreciating the method: the nature of science is considered to be a suitable theme for engaging and challenging the more able in science.

- Authentic enquiry offers opportunities for appreciating the nature of scientific method, as well as the subtleties and complexities of designing experiments and the logical difficulties in drawing sound conclusions from practical work in science.

Summary

- How to plan effectively for science
- Issues relating to appropriate science equipment and resources
- How to use your additional adults to support science learning
- How Inclusion can be promoted in science

- How to challenge children with high learning potential in your classroom
- How the 'More Able' is the phrase now used by Ofsted, the DfE and primary schools when referring to those who are working significantly above national curriculum outcomes.
- How you need to ensure that you know how your school defines the 'Most Able' so that you can identify and provide challenge for the 'Most Able' in your science lessons.
- How it is your responsibility, as the classroom teacher, that all pupils are challenged and make good progress in school; this does not happen by chance, but by carefully planning for the individualized needs of all children in your classroom.

Everything must be made as simple as possible. But not simpler.

Albert Einstein

Recommended reading

Hainsworth, M. (2012). Lifting the Barriers in Science. Primary Science No 125. Available at www.ase.org.uk

Hainsworth, M. (2017). *Developing EAL learners' science conceptual understanding through visualization.* Primary Science No146. Available at: www.ase.org.uk

Key, T. (2012). Science as an Inclusive subject but an exclusive lesson. Primary Science No 125. Available at www.ase.org.uk

Lord, M. (2011). *Asking the right questions.* Primary Science No 117. Available at: www.ase.org.uk

Oswald, S. (2012). Narrowing the gap for children with special educational needs – and others too! Primary Science No 125. Available at www.ase.org.uk

www.mensa.org.uk

www.nace.co.uk

Bibliography

Abrahams, I. and Reiss, M. (2012). Practical work: It's effectiveness in primary and secondary schools in *England. Journal of Research in Science Teaching*, 49(8): 1035–55.

Abrahams, I., Reiss, M. J. and Sharpe, R. (2014). The impact of 'Getting practical work in science' continuing professional development programme on teachers' ideas and practice in science practical work. *Research in Science* and *Technological Education*, 32(3): 263–80.

Alexander, R. (2004). In Pollard, A. (2014). *Readings for Reflective Teaching*. London: Bloomsbury.

Alexander, R. (2017). *Towards Dialogic Teaching – Rethinking Classroom Talk* (5th ed.). Dialogos.

Allen, M. (2014). *Misconceptions in Primary Science* (2nd ed.). Maidenhead: Open University Press.

Allen, M. (2016). *The Best Ways to Teach Primary Science: Research into Practice.* Maidenhead: Open University Press.

Anderson, L. W. and Krathwohl, D. R. (2001). *A Taxonomy for Learning, Teaching and Assessing: A Revision of Bloom's Taxonomy of Educational Objectives.* Boston: Allyn and Bacon.

Archer, L., Osborne, J., Dewitt, J., Dillon, J., Wong, B. and Willis, B. (2013). ASPIRES *Young People and Career Aspirations*, pp. 10–14. London: King's College London.

ASE. (2011). *Be Safe* (4th ed.). Hatfield: Association of Science Education.

Askew, M. (2015). *Transforming Primary Mathematics: Understanding Classroom Tasks, Tools and Talk*. New York: Routledge.

Asoko, H. (2002). In Loxley, P., Dawes, L., Nicholls, L. and Dore, B. (2014). *Teaching Primary Science: Promoting Enjoyment and Developing Understanding*. Abingdon: Routledge.

Assessment Reform Group. (2002). Assessment for Learning: 10 Principles. Available at: http://www.qca.org.uk/libraryAssets/media/4031_afl_principles.pdf.

Aubrey, K. and Riley, A. (2016). *Understanding and Using Educational Theories*. London: Sage.

Berland, K. L. and Hammer, D. (2012). Framing for scientific argumentation. *Journal of Research in Science Teaching*, 49: 68–94.

Biggs, J. B. and Collis, K. F. (1982). *Evaluating the Quality of Learning – the SOLO Taxonomy.* New York: Academic Press.

Black, P. and Wiliam, D. (1998). *Inside the Black Box.* London: nferNelson.

Black, P. and Wiliam, D. (1998). Inside the black box: Raising standards through classroom assessment. *Phi Delta Kappan*, 80(2): 139–48.

Black, P. and Wiliam, D. (2009). Developing the theory of formative assessment. *Educational Assessment, Evaluation and Accountability*, 21(1): 5.

Black, P. J. and Harrison, C. (2004). *Science Inside the Black Box: Assessment for Learning in the Science Classroom.* London: GL Assessment.

Blatchford, P., Bassett, P., Brown, P., Martin, C., Russell, A. and Webster, R., with Babayigit, S. and Haywood, N. (2008). *The Deployment and Impact of Support Staff in Schools and the Impact of the National Agreement: Results from Strand 2 Wave 1 - 2005/6 (DCSF Research Report 027).* London: Department for Children, Schools and Families.

Boaler, J. (2009). *The Elephant in the Classroom: Helping Children Learn and Love Maths.* London: Souvenir. http://primary.cleapss.org.uk/Resources/Doing-Things-Safely/ (accessed 07 May 2017).

Bostrum, C. (2016) *Experiencing Child-led Science in Science Week.* Primary Science No 142. Available at: www.ase.org.uk

Bruner, J. S. (1966). *Towards a Theory of Instruction.* New York: W.W. Norton.

Byrne, J., Ideland, M., Malmberg, C. and Grace, M. (2014). Climate change and everyday life: Repertoires children use to negotiate a socio-scientific issue. *International Journal of Science Education,* 36(9): 1491–509.

CBI. (2014). *Tomorrow's World: Inspiring Primary Scientists.* Available at: https:// www.google.co.uk/webhp?sourceid=chrome-instant&ion=1&espv=2&ie=UTF-8#q=tomorrow%27s%20world%20inspiring%20primary%20scientists

CBI. (2015). *Tomorrow's World: Inspiring Primary Scientists.* London: Brunel University.

Centre for Industry Education Collaboration. Working Scientifically in the Primary Classroom: Progression of Enquiry Skills from EYFS to KS3. Available at: www.ciec.org.uk

CFE. (2017) 'State of the nation' report of UK primary science education – baseline research for the Wellcome Trust Primary Science Campaign. CFE.

Chin, C. (2004). Students' questions: Fostering a culture of inquisitiveness in science classrooms. *School Science Review,* 86(314): 107–12.

Clair, H. and Holden, C. (2007). *The Challenge of Teaching Controversial Issues.* Stoke-on-Trent: Trentham Books Limited.

Clarke, S. (2014). *Outstanding Formative Assessment: Culture and Practice.* London: Hodder Education.

Coe, R., Aloisi, C., Higgins, S. and Major, L. E. (2014). *What Makes Great Teaching? A Review of the Underpinning Research.* The Sutton Trust. Available at: http://www.suttontrust.com/ wp-content/uploads/2014/10/What-makes-great-teaching-FINAL-4.11.14.pdf

Collins, S. (2015). *Neuroscience for Learning and Development: How to Apply Neuroscience and Psychology for Improved Learning and Training.* London: Kogan Page.

Craft, A. (2001). Little c creativity. In A. Craft, B. Jeffrey and M. Leibling (eds.), *Creativity in Education.* London: Continuum.

Craft, A. (2005). *Creativity in Schools: Tensions and Dilemmas.* Abingdon: Routledge.

Creative Scotland. (2013). Available at: http://www.creativescotland.com

Cridland, J. (2015). cited by CBI (2015) *Tomorrow's World: Inspiring Primary Scientists.* Brunel University London.

Cross, A. and Board, J. (2014). *Creative Ways to Teach Primary Science.* Maidenhead: Open University Press.

Cross, A. and Bowden, A. (2014). *Essential Primary Science* (2nd ed.). Maidenhead: Open University Press.

Cutting, R. and Kelly, O. (2015). *Creative Teaching in Primary Science.* London: Sage.

Dairianathan, A. and Subramaniam, R. (2011). Learning about inheritance in an out-of-school setting. *International Journal of Science Education,* 33(8): 1079–108.

Darwin, C. (1859). *On the Origin of Species by Means of Natural Selection.* London: John Murray.

Davies, D. (2011). *Teaching Science Creatively.* Abingdon: Routledge.

Dawson, V. and Venville, G. (2013). Introducing high school biology students to argumentation about socio-scientific issues. *Canadian Journal of Science, Mathematics and Technology Education,* 13(4): 356–72.

DCSF. (2007). *Gender and Education Mythbusters – Addressing Gender and Achievement, Myths and Realities.* Available at: http://webarchive.nationalarchives. gov.uk/20130401151715/http://www.education.gov.uk/publications/ eOrderingDownload/00599-2009BKT-EN.pdf

DCSF. (2008). *Identifying Gifted and Talented Leaners – Getting Started.* Available at: http:// webarchive.nationalarchives.gov.uk/20130401151715/http://www.education.gov.uk/ publications/eOrderingDownload/Getting%20StartedWR.pdf

De Jong, T., van Gog, T., Jenks, K., Manlove, S., van Hell, J., Jolles, J., van Merrienboer, J., van Leeuwan, T. and Bosschloo, A. (2009). In *ASE Guide to Primary Science Education*, edited by Harlen, W. (2011). Hatfield: The Association for Science Education.

DfE. (2012). *Teachers' Standards*. https://www.gov.uk/government/publications/teachers-standards (accessed 3 January 2017).

DfE. (2013). *The National Curriculum in England: Key Stages 1 and 2 Framework Document*. Available at: https://www.gov.uk/government/publications/national-curriculum-in-england-primary-curriculum

DfE. (2013). *Science Programmes of Study: Key Stage 1 and Key Stage 2*. Available at: https://www.gov.uk/government/.../PRIMARY_national_curriculum_-_Science.pdf

Driscoll, P., Lambrith, A. and Roden, J. (2015). *The Primary Curriculum: A Creative Approach*. London: Sage.

Dunne, M. and Makland, R. (2015). In Dunne, M. and Peacock, A., eds (2015). *Primary Science: A Guide to Teaching Practice* (2nd ed.). London: Sage.

Dunne, M. and Peacock, A., eds (2015). *Primary Science: A Guide to Teaching Practice* (2nd ed.). London: Sage.

Duschl, R. A., Scweingruber, H. A. and Shouse, A. W., eds (2007). *Taking Science to School: Learning and Teaching Science in Grades K-8*. Washington DC: National Academies Press.

Dweck, C. (2006). *Mindset: The New Psychology of Success*. New York: Random House Incorporated.

Dweck, C. (2008). *Mindsets and Maths/Science Achievement*. Available at: www.opportunityequation.org

Dweck, C. (2012, 2017). *Mindset – Updated Edition: Changing the Way You Think to Fulfil Your Potential*. London: Robinson.

Education Endowment Foundation. (2016). *Rochdale Research into Practice*. Available at: https://educationendowmentfoundation.org.uk/evaluation/projects/research-into-practice-evidence-informed-cpd-in-rochdale/

Eley, A. (2016). How the 'I can explain!' project helps children learn science through talk. Primary Science No 142. Available at: www.ase.org.uk Forest School Association: www.forestschoolassociation.org/what-is-forest-school

Evagorou, M. (2008). *Technoskepsi Project Report*. Cyprus.

Farrow, S. (2006, 2012). *The Really Useful Science Book: A Framework of Knowledge for Primary Teachers* (3rd ed.). London: Falmer Press.

Farrow, S. and Strachan, A. (2017). *The Really Useful Science Book: A Framework of Knowledge for Primary Teachers* (4th ed.). London: Routledge.

Feasey, R. (2005). *Creative Science: Achieving the WOW Factor with 5–11 Year Olds*. London: David Fulton.

Fleming, M. and Dillon, J. (2017). *Education in Science*, 268: 15

FPA (2011). Sex and relationships education factsheet. Available at: http://www.fpa.org.uk/factsheets/sex-and-relationships-education

Gagne, F. (1999). My convictions about the nature of abilities, gifts and talents. *Journal for the Education of the Gifted*, 22(2): 109–36.

Gershon, M. (2016). *50 Quick Ways to stretch and Challenge More Able Children*. Quick 50 Teaching Series.

Glauert, E., Cremin, T., Craft, A., Compton, A. and Stylianidou, F. (2015). Creative little scientists: Exploring pedagogical synergies between inquiry-based and creative approaches in early years science. *Education 3–13*, 43: 404–19.

Hainsworth, M. (2012). *Lifting the Barriers in Science*. Primary Science No 125. Available at www.ase.org.uk

Hainsworth, M. (2017). *Developing EAL Learners' Science Conceptual Understanding Through Visualization*. Primary Science No 146. Available at: www.ase.org.uk.

Hardman, S. and Luke, S. (2016). *How Can You Make the Most of Those 'Wow moments'?* Primary Science No 141. Available at: www.ase.org.uk

Hargreaves, E. (2007). The validity of collaborative assessment for learning. *Assessment in Education*, 6(1): 129–44.

Harlen, W. (2009). Teaching and learning science for a better future. *School Science Review*, 90(333): 33–41.

Harlen, W., ed. (2010). *Principles and Big Ideas of Science Education*. Hatfield: Association for Science Education.

Harlen, W. and Qualter, A. (2014). *The Teaching of Science in Primary Schools* (6th ed.). London: Routledge.

Harlock, J., Naylor, S. and Moules, J. (2015). *Let's Talk about Evolution.* Millgate House.

Hattie, J. (2012). *Visible Learning for Teachers*. London: Routledge

Hoath, L. (2008). *Does 'Why' Matter?* Primary Science No 105. Available at: www.ase.org.uk

Hodgson, C. and Pyle, K. (2010). *A Literature Review of Assessment for Learning in Science.* Slough: NFER.

Hodson, D. (2008). *Towards Scientific Literacy. A Teacher's Guide to the History, Philosophy and Sociology of Science.* Rotterdam: Sense Publishers.

Holligan, B. (2013). Giving children ownership of their investigations is easier than you might think. *Primary Science*, 128: 5–8.

House of Commons: Children, Schools and Families Committee. (2009). *National curriculum: Fourth report of session 2008-09.* Available at: http://www.publications. parliament.uk/pa/cm200809/cmselect/cmchilsch/344/344i.pdf

Howard, S. (2011). In *ASE Guide to Science Education*, edited by Harlen, W. Hatfield: The Association for Science Education.

Howe, C. and Mercer, N. (2007). Primary Review Research Survey 2/1b: Children's social development, peer interaction and classroom learning. Available at: www.primaryreview. org.uk

Hymer, B. and Hailstone, P. (2009). *Gifted and Talented Pocketbook*. Management Pocketbooks.

Kali, Y., Linn, M. C. and Roseman, J. E., eds (2008). *Designing Coherent Science Education: Implications for Curriculum, Instruction, and Policy*, pp. 185–200. New York: Teachers' College Press.

Keogh, B., Naylor, S., Downing, B., Maloney, J. and Simon, S. (2006). *PUPPETS Bringing Stories to Life in Science.* Primary Science No 92. Available at: www.ase.org.uk

Key, T. (2012). *Science as an Inclusive Subject but an Exclusive Lesson.* Primary Science No 125. Available at: www.ase.org.uk

Kolstø, S. D. (2006). Patterns in students' argumentation confronted with a risk-focused socio-scientific issue. *International Journal of Science Education*, 28(14): 1689–716.

Kumar, D. (2017). *Let's Turn Things on their Head – Teaching Counterintuitive Science.* Primary Science No 148. Available at: www.ase.org.uk

Leroi, A. M. (2014). *The Lagoon, how Aristotle Invented Science.* London: Bloomsbury.

Levinson, R. (2006). Towards a theoretical framework for teaching controversial socio-scientific issues. *International Journal of Science Education*, 28(10): 1201–24.

Levinson, R. and Reiss, M. J., eds (2003). *Key Issues in Bioethics: A Guide for Teachers.* London: Routledge-Falmer.

Levy, P., Lameras, P., McKinney, P. and Ford, N. (2011). *The Pathway to Inquiry Based Science Teaching.* Available at: www.pathwayuk.org. uk/uploads/9/3/2/1/9321680/_the_features_of_inquiry_learning__theory_research_and_ practice_eusubmitted.pdf.

Lord, M. (2011). *Asking the Right Questions.* Primary Science No 117. Available at: www. ase.org.uk

Loxley, P. and Dawes, L. (2013). *Teaching Primary Science: Promoting Enjoyment and Developing Understanding.* London: Routledge.

Loxley, P., Dawes, L., Nicholls, L. and Dore, B. (2013). *Teaching Primary Science - Promoting Enjoyment and Developing Understanding* (2nd ed.). London: Routledge.

McCrory, P. (2011). Developing interest in science through emotional engagement. In *ASE Guide to Primary Science Education*, edited by Harlen, W., pp. 94–101. Hatfield: ASE.

Mercer, N. (1995). *The Guided Construction of Knowledge: Talk Amongst Teachers and Learners.* Clevedon: Multilingual Matters.

Mercer, N., Dawes, L., Wegerif, R. and Sams, C. (2004). Reasoning as a scientist: Ways of helping children to use language to learn science. *British Educational Research Journal*, 30(3): 359–77.

Millar, R. (2007). Twenty-first century science: Insights from the design and implementation of a scientific literacy approach in school science. *International Journal of Science Education*, 28(13): 1499–522.

Murphy, C., Beggs, J. and Russell, H. (2005). *Primary Horizons: Starting out in Science.* London: Wellcome Trust.

Myers, D., McGrory, M. and Westgate, C. (2016). *Curiouser and Curiouser: Supporting Children's Independent Enquiry Skills.* Primary Science No 142. Available at: www.ase.org.uk

NACE. (2016). Leading and teaching for able, gifted and talented pupils. Available at: http://www.nace.co.uk/sites/default/files/resources

National Advisory Committee on Creative and Cultural Education. (1999). *All Our Futures: Creativity, Culture and Education.* London: NACCCE. Available at: http://sirkenrobinson.com/pdf/allourfutures.pdf

National Research Council. (2005). Available at: http://www.rcuk.ac.uk (accessed 12 November 2016).

Naylor, S. and Keogh, B. (2000). *Concept Cartoons in Science Education.* Sandbach: Millgate House Publishers.

Nottingham, J. and Nottingham, J. (2017). *Challenging Learning Through Feedback: How to Get the Type, Tone and Quality of Feedback Right Every Time.* Challenging Learning. Thousand Oaks: Sage.

Ofsted. (2011). *Successful Science: An Evaluation of Science Education in England 2007-2010.* London: Ofsted Publications.

Ofsted. (2011). *Successful Science; Strengths and Weaknesses of School Science Teaching.* Available at: https://www.gov.uk/government/publications/successful-science-strengthes-and-weaknesses-of-school-science-teaching

Ofsted. (2013a). *Maintaining Curiosity; A Survey to Science Education in Schools.* Available at: https://www.gov.uk/government/publications/maintaining-curiosity-a-survey-into-science-education-in-schools

Ofsted. (2013b). *Not Yet Good Enough; Persona; Social, Health and Economic Education on Schools.* Manchester: Ofsted.

Ofsted. (2015). School Inspection Handbook. Available at: https://www.gov.uk/government/publications/school-inspection-handbook-from-september-2015

Oliver, A. (2006). *Creative Teaching: Science in the Early Years and Primary Classroom.* Reprinted 2008, Abingdon: Routledge.

ONS. (2015). More children using social media report mental ill-health symptoms. ONS Digital. Available at: http://visual.ons.gov.uk/more-than-a-quarter-of-children-who-spend-longer-on-social-networking-websites-report-mental-ill-health-symptoms

Oswald, S. (2012). *Narrowing the Gap for Children with Special Educational Needs – and Others Too!* Primary Science No 125. Available at: www.ase.org.uk

Oulton, C., Dillon, J. and Grace, M. (2004). Reconceptualizing the teaching of controversial issues. *International Journal of Science Education*, 26(4): 411–423.4

Peacock, A. (2008). *When Do Children Ask the Really Big Questions?* Primary Science No 105. Available at: www.ase.org.uk

Pell, A. and Jarvis, T. (2003). Developing attitude to science education scales for use with primary teachers. *International Journal of Science Education*, 25(10): 1273–95.

Perry, W. G. (1999). *Forms of Ethical and Intellectual Development.* San Francisco: Jossey-Bass Publishers.

Piaget, J. (1929). *The Child's Conception of the World.* London: Harcourt Bruce.

Piaget, J. (1961). In Colwell, J. and Pollard, A. (2015). *Readings for Reflective Teaching in Early Education.* London: Bloomsbury.

Piaget, J. (1972). *The Psychology of the Child.* New York: Basic Books.

Piaget, J. (1973). *Memory and Intelligence.* New York: Basic Books.

Phethean, K. (2008). *When Are You Too Old to 'play' in Science.* Primary Science No 105. Available at: www.ase.org.uk

PHSE Association. (2012). Available at: https://www.pshe-association.org.uk/news/response-nspcc-and-children%E2%80%99s-commissioner-report

Pollard, A. (2014). *Readings for Reflective Teaching.* New York: Sage.

Reuters (2016). Female researchers underrepresented, but collaborate widely. Available at: http://www. reuters.com/article/us-health- research-women-scientists/female-researchers-underrepresented-but-collaborative-widely-idUSKBN1343JZ

Rivett, A. C., Harrison, T. G. and Shallcross, D. E. (2009). *The Art of Chemistry.* Primary Science No 110. Available from www.ase.org.uk

Roden, J. and Archer, J. (2014). *Primary Science for Trainee Teachers.* Newcastle upon Tyne: Sage.

Royal Society. (2010). *Primary Science and Mathematics Education – Getting the Basics Right.* London: Royal Society.

Russell, A., Webster, R. and Blatchford, P. (2013). *Maximising the Impact of Teaching Assistants: Guidance for School Leaders and Teachers.* London: Routledge.

Russell, T. and McGuigan, L. (2016). *Exploring Science with Young Children.* London: Sage.

Rutledge, N. (2010). *Primary Science: Teaching the Tricky Bits.* London: Open University Press.

Sadler, T. D. (2011). *Socio – Scientific Issues in the Classroom: Teaching, Learning and Research.* the Netherlands: Springer.

Sadler, T. D., Romine, W. L. and Topçu, M. S. (2016). Learning science content through socio-scientific issues-based instruction: A multi-level assessment study. *International Journal of Science Education*, 38(10): 1622–35.

Scotland. (2013). What is creativity? A source of inspiration and summary of actions from Scotland's Creative Learning Partners [Online]. Available at: www.creativescotland.com

Sewell, K. (2014). *Primary Science, Teaching Theory and Practice.* London: Learning Matters; Sage.

Sewell, K. (2015). *Planning the Primary National Curriculum.* London: Learning Matters; Sage.

Shakespeare, D. (2003). Starting an argument in science lessons. *School Science Review*, 85: 103–8.

Sharp, J. G., Hopkin, H. and Lewthwaite, B. (2011). Teacher perceptions of science in the national curriculum: Findings from an application of the science curriculum implementation questionnaire in English primary schools. *International Journal of Science Education*, 33(17): 2407–36.

Shulman, A. and Valcarcel, J. (2012). Scientific knowledge suppresses but does not supplant earlier intuitions. *Cognition*, 124(2): 209–15

Shulman, L. S. (1986). In Nuangchalerm, P. (2012). Enhancing pedagogical content knowledge in preservice science teachers. *Higher Education Studies*, 2(2): 66–71.

Shulman, L. S. (2015). PCK: Its genesis and exodus. In *Re-Examining Pedagogical Content Knowledge in Science Education*, edited by Berry, A., Friedrichsen, P. and Loughran, J., pp. 3–13. New York: Routledge.

Silver, A. and Rushton, B. S. (2008). Primary-school children's attitudes towards science, engineering and technology and their images of scientists and engineers. *Education 3–13* 36, 51–67.

Simon, S., Johnson, S., Cavell, S. and Parsons, T. (2012). Promoting argumentation in primary science contexts: An analysis of students' interactions in formal and informal learning environments. *Journal of Computer Assisted Learning*, 28(5): 440–53.

Skamp, K. and Preston, C. (2014). *Teaching Primary Science Constructively.* Melbourne: Cengage Learning Australia.

SPACE (Science processes and concepts exploration). (1990–1998). Liverpool: University of Liverpool Press.

Tal, T., Kali, Y., Magid, S. and Madhok, J. J. (2011). Enhancing the authenticity of a web-based module for teaching simple inheritance. In T. D. Sadler (ed.), S*ocio-Scientific Issues in the Classroom: Teaching, Learning and Research,* Contemporary trends and issues in science education, vol. 39. Dordrecht: Springer.

Tunnicliffe, C. (2010). *Teaching Able, Gifted and Talented Children: Strategies, Activities and Resources.* London: Sage.

Tunnicliffe, S. D. (2015). *Starting Inquiry Based Science in the Early Years – Look, Talk, Think and Do.* London: Taylor Francis.

Turner, J., Keogh, B., Naylor, S. and Lawrence, L. (2011). *It's Not Fair – or is it?* Hatfield: Millgate House Publishers, Sandbach and Association for Science Education.

Van Aalderen-Smeets, S. and Walma van der Molen, J. (2013). Measuring primary teachers' attitudes toward teaching science: Development of the dimensions of attitude toward science (DAS) *Instrument, International Journal of Science Education,* 35(4): 577–600.

Van Biema, D. (2005). Can you believe in god and evolution? *Time,* 166: 34–5.

Veall, D. (2015). University museums, a space for inquiry. *School Science Review, September 2015,* 97: 358.

Vygotsky, L. (1978). *Language and Thought.* Ontario, Canada: MIT Press.

Vygotsky, L. (1978). *Mind in Society: Development of Higher Psychological Processes.* Cambridge, MA: Harvard University Press.

Ward, H. and Remnant, K. (2016). In Ward, H. and Roden, J. (2016). *Teaching Science in the Primary Classroom.* London: Sage.

Wellcome (2015) A review of Ofsted Inspection reports: Science. Available at: https://wellcome.ac.uk/sites/defualt/files/review-of-ofsted-inspection-reports-wellcome-dec16.pdf

Wellcome Trust. (2013). *Primary Science, Is It Missing Out?* London: Wellcome Trust.

Wellcome Trust. (2014). *Primary Science: Is It Missing Out? Recommendations for Reviving Primary Science.* Available at: https://wellcome.ac.uk/sites/default/files/primary-science-is-it-missing-out-wellcome-sep14.pdf

Wellcome Trust. (2016). *NFER Teacher Voice Survey Data.* Available at: https://wellcome.ac.uk/sites/default/files/nfer-teacher-voice-omnibus-survey-data-apr16.pdf

Wellington, J. J., ed. (1986). *Controversial Issues in the Curriculum.* Blackwell: Oxford.

Wesley, L. (2017). *Add More Gin! Common Misconceptions and Strategies for Correcting Them.* Primary Science No 148. Available at: www.ase.org.uk

Wiliam, D. (2008). *Chapter 9; Content, then Process: Teacher Learning Communities in the Service of Formative Assessment, in D. Reeves (2008) Ahead of the Curve*: The Power to Transform Teaching and Learning. Solution Tree.

Women and Equalities Committee (2016). *Sexual Harassment and Sexual Violence Inquiry in Schools.* Available at: https://www.parliament.uk/business/committees/committees-a-z/commons-select/women-and-equalities-committee/inquiries/parliament-2015/inquiry1/

Wood, D., Bruner, J. and Ross, G. (1976). In Wood, D. (1988). *How Children Think and Learn.* Oxford: Blackwell.

Woolley, R. (2010). *Tackling Controversial Issues in the Primary School: Facing Life's Challenges with Your Learners.* London: Routledge.

Wurman, R. S. (2000). *Information Anxiety 2.* Indianapolis: QUE

Wyse, D. and Dowson, P. (2009). *The Really Useful Creativity Book.* London: Routledge.

Yeager, D. S. and Dweck, C. S. (2012). Mindsets that promote resilience: When students believe that personal characteristics can be developed. *Educational Psychologist,* 47(4): 302–14.

Index